Women
Leaders in
Contemporary
U.S. Politics

Women Leaders in Contemporary U.S. Politics

edited by
Frank P. Le Veness & Jane P. Sweeney

Lynne Rienner Publishers • Boulder & London

Published in the United States of America in 1987
by Lynne Rienner Publishers, Inc.
948 North Street, Boulder, Colorado 80302

Library of Congress Cataloging-in-Publication Data

Women leaders in contemporary U.S. politics.

Bibliography: p.
Includes index.
Contents: American women and political success /
F. P. Le Veness and J. P. Sweeney—Shirley Chisholm /
Reba Carruth—Dianne Feinstein / Kirsten Amunsden—
[etc.].
    1. Women in politics—United States—Biography.
2. Women in politics—United States.   I. Le Veness,
Frank P. (Frank Paul)   II. Sweeney, Jane P.
HQ1236.5.U6W666   1987   320′.088042   86-24825
ISBN 0-931477-87-5 (lib. bdg.)
ISBN 0-931477-88-3 (pbk.)

Printed and bound in the United States of America.

The paper used in this publication meets the
requirements of the American National Standard
for Permanence of Paper for Printed Library   ∞
Materials Z39.48-1984.

To our parents,
Regina Le Veness and
Doris and Robert Sweeney,
to the memory of the late
Francis E. Le Veness,
and to the next generation of women,
Kristin Le Veness and Laura and Megan Swanson

Contents

Acknowledgments

Lynne Rienner encouraged this project from the outset and has been a most helpful publisher. We are grateful to her and her able assistant, Crawford Lindsey, and to her staff, especially Dianne Ewing and Gia Hamilton. Graduate assistant Gail L. Glenn tracked down items for the annotated bibliography and served as faithful courier between our two campuses. Gail's organizational skills are much appreciated.

Many of the women we have studied, as well as some of their family members, granted personal interviews to our contributors or provided gracious assistance from their staffs. We thank them for their cooperation. We also wish to acknowledge our contributing authors for the enthusiasm and skill they brought to this project.

Our secretaries on both the Queens and Staten Island campuses of St. John's University helped us in many significant ways. We thank Rose Peragine, Edna Rodgers, Florence Carini, Janet McQuillan, and student-typist Eileen Bermingham.

While in the final stages of getting this book together we neglected our families. Nevertheless, they were patient and supportive as they always are, and we are grateful to them. The understanding support of Kristin A. Le Veness is particularly acknowledged.

Lastly, we wish to acknowledge all the women who have run for political office in this country. We both believe their presence has been of great value to our society.

Frank P. Le Veness
Jane P. Sweeney

Women
Leaders in
Contemporary
U.S. Politics

Women in the Political Arena

FRANK P. Le VENESS and JANE P. SWEENEY

As U.S. political pundits discuss possible 1988 candidates for national office, it is clear that perceptions of women as viable candidates for the vice presidency were changed forever by Walter Mondale's selection of running mate and by Geraldine Ferraro's feisty campaign. Prominent political women of both parties now view themselves as potential candidates for that office and are not shy about seeking it. Although our society does not yet consider a woman in the vice presidential slot a necessity for balancing the ticket, Jeane Kirkpatrick, Nancy Kassebaum, and Elizabeth Dole all have been mentioned as potential Republican party candidates. The Democrats have several prominent women, such as Dianne Feinstein, Patricia Schroeder, and Barbara Mikulski, who are seasoned and nationally recognized politicians.

Although women remain a marginal group in high elected office in this nation (for example, they make up only 2 percent of the members of the U.S. Senate and 4 percent of the U.S. House of Representatives) and, indeed, worldwide, they have become much more visible and have been viewed with steadily increasing respect in recent years. In addition, the present generation of political women provides role models for today's young women, who can now think realistically about being the mayor of a major U.S. city, a justice of the Supreme Court, or, conceivably, president of the United States.

In this brief volume, we study the careers of nine U.S. political women, believing that a biographical approach will lead to insights about how women achieve elite status in politics and what obstacles peculiar to their sex they are forced to confront. In addition, our final chapter examines the vital role of the "unnamed" political women who contribute through their political activism to the quality of life in their local communities.

Obviously, there are many more than nine prominent women in U.S. politics, so a word is in order about our choice of subjects. We believe that two women—Geraldine A. Ferraro and Sandra Day O'Connor—have such

1

historical importance as "firsts" that inclusion of chapters on their lives and accomplishments is vital. Beyond that, we looked for women from both major political parties (and chose four Republicans and five Democrats) who have held or at present hold a variety of public offices, ranging from local to national in scope: Ambassador Margaret Heckler, a former congresswoman and cabinet member; Ambassador Jeane Kirkpatrick, former U.S. permanent representative to the United Nations; Mayor Dianne Feinstein of San Francisco; Senator Nancy Landon Kassebaum of Kansas; Kings County District Attorney Elizabeth Holtzman of Brooklyn, New York, a former member of Congress; former congresswoman Shirley Chisholm; and former member of Congress Barbara Mikulski, who was elected to the U.S. Senate from the State of Maryland in 1986. We truly hope that prominent women not discussed in this volume, and their many supporters, will understand that we were confronted with limitations of space and were forced to make some very difficult choices.

In order to provide some basis for comparison of the careers of these women, we asked the contributors to focus their chapters on three aspects of each subject's life and contributions: such biographical material as is pertinent to the woman's subsequent career path; those issues in which each woman most interested and involved herself during her public career; and the position each woman took on issues of particular importance to women.

Although each of these women is unique, all nine are intelligent, well educated, life-long achievers, and all, even those who did not consider themselves feminists, found themselves being drawn into the debates on women's issues. By "women's issues" we mean public policy decisions which impact more strongly on women than on men. We would include such diverse issues as funding of day care, equal employment opportunities, equality in insurance premiums, financial problems of older women living alone, job training for displaced homemakers, the legality of abortion, and the Equal Rights Amendment. A feminist, as we employ the term, is a woman or man who wants these policy questions decided in a manner that gives women the maximum opportunity to participate fully in our society without discrimination. We might add, as we are dealing here with women politicians, that a feminist politician is one (female or male) who devotes substantial career time to furthering women's issues.

Studying the characteristics these women share may shed some light on what types of women can rise to elite status in U.S. politics.

These women tend to come from families that gave them both support and strong values. Our nine subjects do not share the same economic histories. Some come from affluent families, some from families that struggled quite hard to make ends meet, but all were encouraged toward a self-reliance considered unladylike when they were young. Chisholm's immigrant family from Barbados had to go so far as to send her back to the Caribbean to weather the Great Depression (however, she still credits her family with instilling in her strong community and religious values). Ferraro had some relatives who did not understand why a "nice" girl needed to accept a college scholarship; nevertheless, her mother and grandmother stood firmly by her side. Jeane Kirkpatrick's family weathered the Depression in the Midwest, and her mother, in particular, encouraged Jeane to be anything she desired.

Much of the literature on women in politics cites childhood socialization as a reason women avoid the confrontational world of politics. The parents of these nine women did not particularly guide them into exceptional careers, but it does seem they all were nurtured in environments that engendered a sense of personal efficacy. All nine came into adulthood secure in the knowledge that they could achieve.

Several of the women studied here attribute their current political values to strong religious upbringings. Barbara Mikulski praises the role of the Catholic ethnic parish of her youth. Elizabeth Holtzman was influenced by the social thought of Rabbi Hillel and the atmosphere of the Brooklyn Ethical Culture School. Shirley Chisholm's family were devout members of the Society of Friends (Quakers), and Geraldine Ferraro was deeply influenced by the Catholicism which she and her mother still devoutly practice.

The educational achievements of these women parallel those of men with comparable levels of political success. Every one of these women was a bright student, and each attained a high level of education, especially for women born in the 1920s and 1930s. Many were straight-A students in secondary school as well as editors of newspapers and class officers at a time when women were not expected to do such things, except in all-women educational institutions. College scholarships and *magna cum laude* degrees abound in their records. Every one of them undertook graduate work.

Four of the women—Heckler, Holtzman, Ferraro, and, of course, O'Connor—became lawyers when it was still a rarity for women to be accepted for admission to law schools and to compete successfully in that profession. Holtzman, after graduating from Radcliffe College in 1962, entered Harvard Law as one of fifteen women in a class of five hundred. O'Connor earned her law degree with distinction at Stanford. Heckler, the only woman in her class at Boston College's School of Law, edited the law review and won the moot court competition three times. Ferraro's route through law school was not as straightforward as these others. She first earned her degree in education at Marymount Manhattan, a Catholic women's college, and then attended Fordham University Law School at night while teaching during the day at a New York City public school. (Schools such as Marymount Manhattan and Fordham were—and still are—avenues forward for the upwardly mobile ethnic community of New York.)

Whereas law is a typical route into politics for men, five of these women moved into the public arena along other paths. Kirkpatrick—after a break in her education while she raised her children—earned a doctorate in political science and commenced a successful academic career. Feinstein did graduate work in criminal justice, which led to a career in public service and, finally, public office. Chisholm and Mikulski moved into careers typical of aspiring women of working-class origins. Chisholm, who had turned down scholarships to several prestigious schools because her family could not afford the overhead of a boarding school, graduated from Brooklyn College and did graduate work in education and administration. Mikulski attended a small Catholic women's college in Maryland and then attained a graduate degree in social work. For them and for Feinstein, involvement in the community led to political careers.

These women have learned that the behavioral rules imposed on female politicians are stricter than those imposed on male politicians. One of the women those opposed to the presence of women in the corridors of political power love to hate is Bella Abzug, former congresswoman from New York City, who ran again for office in 1986, but lost. Abzug is a brash and outspoken feminist with a certain ability to go for the jugular, which is often the norm in New York City, but not necessarily in Congress. Feminist supporters of Abzug and lovers of the rough-and-tumble of big city politics may relish her approach, but many political women have learned gradually that political success requires that men not be unnecessarily threatened. Chisholm began her career in the House with a feisty speech against the Vietnam conflict and found that her outspoken views did not serve her well among her party's leadership. Others—Ferraro and Mikulski are good examples—developed personal styles reminiscent of Sam Rayburn's old adage, "To get along, go along." The less abrasive style of many contemporary political women does not mean they have sacrificed their interest in women's issues, simply that they have learned that politics is a game of strategy which men have long known how to play.

Women in public life are still scrutinized for defects that would not be noticed in a male. Their wardrobes must be neither too feminine nor too masculine. Their waistlines and hairstyles are the object of frequent comment. Strength is dubbed shrillness, tenacity is bad temper. And who can forget the ridiculous commentary attending the question of whether Ferraro and Mondale should kiss in public during the 1984 presidential campaign?

The fact that political women must endure prying and criticism to which their male colleagues are not subject is, of course, not fair, but it is a reality women in politics have learned to accept. Possibly, as more women empower themselves at the local level and as men become more accustomed to women's participation across the spectrum of professions, close scrutiny of the personal lives and personalities of political women will decline.

An interesting example of campaign tactics directed against political women but not men is the case of former congresswoman Martha Keyes of Kansas. Keyes divorced her husband while in Congress and married another member of the House. In her next campaign (1978), she was attacked on this point by her opponent, James Jeffries. Jeffries defeated her, and two years later her ex-husband, Sam Keyes, ran against Jeffries. Although Sam Keyes did not win, the divorce was never mentioned during his campaign.[1]

Political women are expected to defer to their roles as mothers and homemakers. During the 1960 presidential campaign Jacqueline Kennedy was pregnant and the mother of a small child. She took on the demanding role of first lady and fulfilled it in an activist style. No one during the campaign or the Kennedy presidency thought it inappropriate that the mother of small children was politically active for the sake of *her husband's* career. Rosalynn Carter was the mother of a young child while she worked as an ambitious first lady and the political confidante of the president. Scores of other political wives have separated themselves from young children to campaign for their husbands. This society does not disapprove in these cases. However, if women run for office themselves, the question of whether they are fulfilling their responsibilities as parents immediately arises. The wife of a governor does not have to be home with her baby, it seems. The wife who aspires to be a governor does!

The result of this attitude is that women tend to get a later start in politics than do men. Mikulski and Holtzman did not face this problem because neither married nor had children. Kirkpatrick did not go back to school to earn her Ph.D. until all her children were in school, and so the career in academic publishing that led to her appointment as ambassador to the United Nations was delayed. Ferraro did not practice law full-time until her children were raised. (Please note, however, that neither of these women has publicly complained about this limitation.) Heckler and O'Connor balanced careers in law with childrearing. Kassebaum assumed no career at all until her children were raised and she and her husband were separated.

The result of the gaps between the time many women finish their formal education and are able to take on political careers without public criticism is critical to women's success in politics. There are women like O'Connor and Kirkpatrick who literally start at the top in politics, but they are exceptions—not unlike senators Bill Bradley and Ted Kennedy. Most political careers begin in local or state office and advance slowly. Mikulski was first elected to the Baltimore City Council at age thirty-five and is now running for the U.S. Senate at age fifty, a time frame typical of a successful male politician. For women who must first raise children, a local political career commences late and the chances of reaching high elected office are thereby diminished.

Women's paths into politics are varied. These nine women achieved political prominence in a variety of ways. It is easy to say that Ronald Reagan needed a women for the U.S. Supreme Court, that Walter Mondale desperately needed a spark for his campaign, that Nancy Landon Kassebaum has a magic name in Kansas—that women who achieve success in politics do so because of luck. It is true that O'Connor and Ferraro and Kirkpatrick were at the right places at the right times, but it is equally true that they bucked the odds to arrive at those places. As for Kassebaum's use of the Landon name, contemporary U.S. politics is replete with males named Rockefeller, Roosevelt, Stevenson, and Kennedy—none hurt by association with famous relatives. Kassebaum, whose famous father at first was ambivalent about her candidacy, had to rely on her own political savvy and connections once she began her race.

Chisholm, Ferraro, and Holtzman all became successes in electoral politics in essentially the same way. They entered Democratic primaries for the House of Representatives in which they challenged the anointed candidates of the local party leaders. They each staged skillful uphill battles—Holtzman unseated an incumbent who was considered invincible by many, Chisholm proved that a black woman could beat the local leaders, and Ferraro soundly defeated the candidate of the Queens County Democratic chairman. (It is interesting to note that Ferraro's former opponent succeeded her as representative of the Queens County Ninth Congressional District.) None of these women got to the U.S. House of Representatives because anyone had paved the way for her.

Feinstein, Mikulski, and Heckler began their careers in local office. True, Feinstein inherited the office of mayor of San Francisco through a tragic assassination, but only because she was already the president of the Board of Supervisors. Heckler began political life as a volunteer in the local Republican club in Wellesley, Massachusetts, and she defied her state party leadership when she entered the Republican primary for the House. Mikulski was the leader of a successful community group who became a popular city council member and then representative.

Once at the elite level, being a women can be advantageous to one's career. Geraldine Ferraro and Sandra Day O'Connor were both refreshingly candid when contributors to this volume asked them how being women affected them when the big opportunities finally came their way. Ferraro thinks that the fact that she was one of a handful of Democratic women in the House and was willing to cooperate with the party's leadership gave her entrance into positions not open to men as junior as she. It was, of course, those leadership positions that led to national prominence as chair of the 1984 Democratic Platform Committee and her eventual selection as Walter Mondale's running mate. O'Connor, when asked if she would be on the Supreme Court today if she were a male, said she did not think so. She pointed out that there were very few Republican women on the federal bench when

Ronald Reagan was searching for a woman suitable to serve as associate justice on the U.S. Supreme Court.

However, lest the reader think this means it is easy for women to advance in the political world, it must be emphasized that women have a very difficult time gaining entrance to circles where the number of women is so small that being one of them might mean opportunity. Even at that level, Jeane Kirkpatrick found the problem of sexism at the United Nations quite difficult. (Even today there are very few female permanent representatives in that august body.) Nancy Kassebaum was first called "nice little Nancy" by other senators. Shirley Chisholm dealt with both racism and sexism during her first campaign, when she arrived in the House, and when she ran for the presidency in 1972.

Positions on women's issues and activity on behalf of women differ considerably in this group. The women discussed in this book are very much individuals, and they cannot be pigeonholed into neat feminist and antifeminist categories. For example, one might try to classify Kassebaum and Heckler as "moderate feminists." What does that mean? Kassebaum favors legalized abortion and voted against extending the deadline for ratification of the Equal Rights Amendment, while Heckler took diametrically opposite stances. Mikulski and Chisholm often have had women's issues high on their political agendas; Feinstein and Kirkpatrick have kept a relatively low profile on women's issues.

However, the positions these women have taken on women's issues—particularly the ERA and the *Roe v. Wade* decision of the U.S. Supreme Court legalizing abortion—arouse intense emotions among those defending both sides of each controversy. Ferraro, a Roman Catholic, has taken the position that as a matter of personal conscience she cannot dictate to others as a legislator. Basically, she assumed a "pro-choice" position in her lawmaking role while continuing to personally oppose abortion. Throughout her legislative career she has had to continually explain and defend her position, and she has been opposed by members of her church's hierarchy (during the post–Labor Day period of her vice presidential campaign) and by various groups of "pro-life" advocates (some of whom have been vociferous in their denunciation of her positions). On other women's issues she has joined the ranks of Mikulski and Chisholm and has placed a high legislative priority on these questions. One of her outstanding achievements in the House was the passage of the private pension bill she had introduced, a bill designed to offer far more equitable treatment to women in the labor force upon their retirement than did many of the programs then in effect.

As a final note, the editors wish to emphasize that one of their primary goals in undertaking this project has been to enlighten readers as to the possibilities and problems facing women who enter the political arena. There are many potential entrants into this arena now that educational and career opportunities have substantially widened for women in the United States. Nevertheless, sexism, like racism, dies slowly. Hurdles must be vaulted, and serious calculations must be undertaken by women who seek to reach political heights. We hope that this book will inspire young women to pursue careers in politics and women of all ages to participate actively in the political process. The opportunities are challenging and exciting, and the nation cannot afford to waste the wisdom, talent, and energy of its female citizens.

Note

1. Jane Sweeney lived in Kansas in 1980, participated in Sam Keyes's campaign, and learned the oral history of the 1978 race.

Shirley Chisholm: Woman of Complexity, Conscience, and Compassion

REBA CARRUTH and VIVIAN JENKINS NELSEN

Life Forces and Personal Choices

Shirley St. Hill Chisholm's rise to national prominence in the U.S. political system was an astounding achievement for a woman and for a person of color. She was the first black woman to be elected to Congress. The national attention she received reached a peak in 1972 when she mounted a bid for the presidency. Indeed, her sex, her black skin, and foreign parentage caused the most progressive segments of society to question Chisholm's potential as a political leader in a traditionally white, male-dominated arena. However, her pioneering challenge to racist and sexist biases inherent in the U.S. political system led the way for other black women congressional leaders to begin remedying the underrepresentation of black women in the policymaking process.

The unique personal and professional strengths that undergird Chisholm's impressive career as a public servant have their roots in her humble, strictly disciplined childhood. Born to parents who immigrated from Barbados and Guiana, Chisholm was endowed with a strong sense of ethnic pride, which was perhaps why she was able to violate the implicit and explicit behavior codes that had historically prevented many U.S.-born blacks from excelling. (In fact, Chisholm cites the early liberation of black slaves in Barbados and their strong commercial skills as determining factors in their success relative to blacks born in the United States.)

A strong family network in Barbados and in New York reinforced ideals inculcated by Chisholm's parents, who prized the British values of education, individual initiative, and entrepreneurship. Despite the shared values, Chisholm's father rejected "the divine right of kings" and scorned the inher-

9

ent racism of British colonialism. Instead, Chisholm said, her father chose to be "a follower of Marcus Garvey, the Jamaican who originated many of the ideas that characterize today's militant black separatists."[1] Garvey's 1920's declaration that "black is beautiful" was part of his attempt to unite U.S. blacks and return them to Africa where in independent isolation they would become the equals of any men and women. Chisholm wrote, "I think this appealed to my father because he too, was a very proud black man. He instilled pride in his children, a pride in ourselves and our race that was not as fashionable at that time as it is today."[2] Chisholm's parents emphasized education, professional success, and poise. The strong work ethic stressed by her extended family was reinforced by the teachings and ethics of the Quaker church in which she received religious and spiritual guidance during her youth in New York and during extended visits to Barbados. The impact of these forces is reflected in her choice of vocations and her indefatigable service for human rights, equal opportunity, and community development.

The racially changing Brooklyn community in which Chisholm was reared was also catalytic in forming her understanding of systemic racism. Blacks from the U.S. South were migrating northward to find jobs at the Brooklyn Navy Yard as well as in the Long Island aircraft plants and other growing defense industries.

> No one knew it then, but the present-day "inner city" (to use a white euphemism) was being created. Black workers had to crowd into neighborhoods that were already black or partly so, because they could not find homes anywhere else. Buildings that had four apartments suddenly had eight, and bathrooms that had been private were shared. White building inspectors winked at housing code violations and illegal rates of occupancy, white landlords doubled and trebled their incomes on slum buildings, and the white neighborhoods in other parts of town and in the suburbs stayed white. Today's urban ghettos were being born.[3]

During Chisholm's grade school years, though her parents lived and worked in the New York area, the Depression forced them to send their three girls back home to stay with relatives in Barbados. There, Chisholm and her two sisters spent four

> barefoot, winterless years.... When we came home, the first thing we had to do was take off our school clothes, which were issued clean on Monday and had to stay that way through Friday. Then we carried the water and helped with the other chores, feeding the chickens and ducks, gathering eggs, changing the straw bedding for the cattle and sheep.[4]

The girls were reunited with their parents in Brooklyn in 1934, and Chisholm faced a setback at Public School 84 on Glenmore Avenue. Just before she left Barbados, she had been promoted to the sixth form, so I expected to be put in the sixth grade in Brooklyn . . . the teachers were satisfied with my reading and writing ability, but horrified by my ignorance of American history and geography. They put me in grade 3-B, with children two years younger than I was. Bored, I became a discipline problem. I carried rubber bands in the pocket of my middy blouse and snapped them at the other children; I became expert at making spitballs and flicking them when the teacher's back was turned. Luckily someone diagnosed the trouble and did something about it. The school provided me with a tutor in American geography and history for a year and a half, until I caught up with and passed my age-grade level.[5]

Throughout her high school years Shirley Chisholm excelled academically but the educational options available to her were constricted by the racial and sexual bias of the war years. She attended the highly regarded Girls' High School, one of Brooklyn's oldest schools, where she won a medal in French and was vice president of the honor society. Chisholm was offered scholarships to Oberlin and to Vassar, but her parents could not afford room and board at an out-of-town school, so she entered Brooklyn College. Although women had never been elected to campus office, Chisholm set about helping two young women make a run for the Student Council presidency (which was unsuccessful). Blacks were not welcome in campus social clubs, so she and some friends formed a black women's student's society which she named "Ipothia" an acronym for "in pursuit of the highest in all." Despite Chisholm's efforts, the harsh reality of racism in higher education and the systematic exclusion of blacks and women from vocations in medicine, science, and law severely limited her choice of professions—in fact, blacks were not even permitted to enter the social work professions as late as the 1940s. Chisholm chose early childhood education and school administration as her first profession. After graduating from Columbia University with a B.A. and an M.A. in education and a diploma in administration, she began her career as a school teacher and later assumed the directorship of a day care center. In 1959 she left the Hamilton-Madison Center to become a consultant to the City Division of Day Care; she was responsible for the supervision of ten day care centers as well as setting standards for child care in New York City.

Although women traditionally have chosen careers in education and nursing by default or for lack of other options, often their lives subsequently have shaped these choices in provocative, often fruitful ways. Chisholm's work in elementary education and school administration reinforced her intention to fight ignorance and poverty at all levels of society. Her increased awareness of the effects of poverty and inequality led her to become an active volunteer in the Twelfth Congressional District of Brooklyn. Chisholm's participation in local politics gave her a practical education in the working process of the Democratic party and sharpened her ability to turn ideas and beliefs into votes. The turning point in her professional life came when Louis Warsoff, a blind political science professor, told her that given her strong debating skills and analytical mind she should go into politics. Chisholm reminded the professor that she was black and female, and therefore had no chance of being elected for campus offices, let alone public office, but Warsoff's encouragement gave her the "push" that was needed to enter the political arena.

Shirley Chisholm's successful early participation in voter registration drives, Democratic party fund raisers, and election campaigns quickly led to a test by fire when she challenged the white male political machine in the Twelfth Congressional District in Brooklyn. In the early phase of her political career, Shirley Chisholm fought diligently on behalf of working-class citizens in her district. Although many of her battles with the Democratic machine centered around the party's failure to serve as advocate for the majority of Puerto Rican and black voters in her district, the largest and most intense confrontations arose over the disenfranchisement of working-class people from the political process. Chisholm entered public office to make the system accessible to the entire U.S. population.

Chisholm's color, sex and foreign parentage worked against easy access to political power. At the time of her entry into local politics, the Democratic and Republican clubs were the focal points of party organization. In theory, the goal of these clubs was to provide community advocacy services for local constituents, such as legal services for the poor, selection of candidates to run for public office, and so on. But these clubs excluded women and minorities from decisionmaking positions and often barred them from serving as official representatives of their districts.

The 1960s and 1970s were critical years for Shirley Chisholm's political career. During this period, Chisholm gained a reputation as a maverick and troublemaker, qualities that later aided her in effectively challenging the inequities in the political system. With the support of progressive white and black voters, Chisholm formed the Unity Democratic Club as an alternative to the existing political machine in Brooklyn. The goal of this organization was to mobilize the predominately black and Puerto Rican district in order to facilitate political change and true community development. The first major victory of this "rainbow coalition" was the election of Thomas R. Jones as the first black assemblyman from the Twelfth Congressional District of Brooklyn. This political victory was overshadowed by Chisholm's own nomination and successful campaign for the position of state representative of the district—an achievement astonishing in light of the powerful resistance of males, both black and white, to her nomination for this position. In fact, racism within the Democratic party, from liberal as well as conservative groups, and sexism on the part of white and black men proved to be challenging life forces throughout her long career as a public official. Nevertheless, personal choices—to pursue a college degree; to enter politics as a candidate rather than as a support worker; to not be cowed by withering resistance, whatever its source; to seek and embody excellence in all her endeavors—enabled Chisholm to challenge racist and sexist barriers.

The Good Fight

Elected to the Ninety-first Congress in 1969, Shirley Chisholm was preceded by her reputation as an unpredictable black and an uncontrollable woman. Chisholm's maiden speech in Congress late in March did little to dispel this notion. The major themes of her campaign included jobs, job training, equality education, adequate housing, enforcement of antidiscrimination laws, support for day care centers, and the end of the Vietnam War. As she prepared for her maiden speech in Congress, President Nixon announced that the United States would not be safe until an ABM system was built, and that the Head Start program in the District of Columbia was to be cut back for lack of money. Although not a pacifist, Chisholm felt that it was wrong to spend billions on an elaborate weapons system when disadvantaged children were getting nothing. In a now famous speech she challenged the Nixon administration.

> We Americans have to feel that it is our mission to make the world free. We believe we are good guys at home, too. When the Kerner Commission told white America what black America has always known, that prejudice and hatred built the nation's slums, maintains them and profits by them, white Americans could not believe it. But it is true. Unless we start to fight and defeat the enemies in our own country, poverty and racism, and make our talk of equality and opportunity ring true, we are exposed in the eyes of the world as hypocrites when we talk about making people free.
>
> I am deeply disappointed at the clear evidence that the number one priority of the new administration is to buy more and more and more weapons of war, to return to the era of the Cold War and to ignore the war we must fight here, the war that is not optional. There is only one way, I believe, to turn these policies around. The Congress must respond to the mandate that the American people have clearly expressed. They have said, "End this war. Stop the waste. Stop the killing. Do something for our own people first."[6]
>
> We must force the administration to rethink its distorted, unreal scale of priorities. Our children, our jobless men, our deprived, rejected, and starving fellow citizens must come first. For this reason, I intend to vote "no" on every money bill that comes to the floor of this House that provides any funds for the Department of Defense. Any bill whatsoever, until the time comes when our values and priorities have been turned right-side up

again, until the monstrous waste and the shocking profits in the defense budget have been eliminated and our country starts to use its strength, its tremendous resources, for people and peace, not for profits and war.[7]

As she walked out of the House chamber, she overheard one member say to another, "You know, she's crazy!" Later other colleagues told her that she had been politically unwise to air such views when the nation was at war. Therefore, it is not surprising that her male colleagues attempted to use her rookie status in Congress to crush her strong spirit and to send a message to the growing masses of "pushy" blacks and "uppity" women. Many of her male colleagues were surprised to find her a truly reflective and compassionate human being who was well suited to formulate national policies in a wide variety of social and economic sectors. But this realization on the part of many new and elder statesmen did not prevent them from harassing her. The first test was her assignment to the Agriculture Committee. Chisholm's assignment to this committee, especially to forestry projects, was inappropriate in light of her strong background in urban affairs and was a source of amusement to many of her colleagues. In spite of her efforts to quietly resolve this problem, elder statesmen such as Wilbur Mills initially responded with patronizing statements designed to keep Chisholm "in her place." In fact, Mills, who headed the committee, reacted angrily to her continued requests for reassignment, telling Chisholm to be a "good soldier." After all attempts to silence her failed and the press rallied to her defense, Chisholm won reassignment to the Veterans Committee. In this post, she aided the large numbers of war veterans in her district and in the country. Although this was a small victory in the eyes of some of her political contemporaries, the incident sent a warning to many of her political enemies who had underestimated her ability to win a principled fight against powerful political adversaries.

Chisholm's congressional career was shaped by the needs of her constituents. Early in her legislative career she wrote,

I did not come to Congress to behave myself and stay away from explosive issues so I can keep coming back. Under the circumstances, it's hard for me to imagine I will stay here long. There isn't much that I can do inside Congress in a legislative way. There is a great deal I can do for the people of my district by using my office and the resources it opens up to me in helping individuals and groups. I can investigate the unfair treatment of a black sergeant in the air force, and I can help a black businessman in Brooklyn apply for a Small Business Administration loan, and do so successfully in a satisfying number of cases. This kind of work is important and it occupies a lot of my time and most of the time of my staff. But beyond that, my most valuable function, I think, is as a voice. The accident of my prominence at this period in the struggle of my race for justice and equality can be a good thing if I use it well. I work to be a major force for change outside the House, even if I cannot be one within it. I still believe that our system of representative government can work. It deserves another chance. I feel change will come sooner or later.[8]

In the second year in her term in Congress, a new abortion reform organization called the National Association for the Repeal of Abortion Laws (NARAL), based in New York City, asked her to lead its campaign for the repeal of all laws restricting abortion. Chisholm declined the presidency of NARAL, citing a lack of time, but made television appearances supporting the NARAL campaign. Many black leaders did not support her position on abortion because they felt that even birth control and family planning clinics were thinly veiled attempts by the white power structure to limit the number of blacks; these leaders labeled such programs "genocide." Chisholm responded,

> Women know, and so do many men, that two or three children who are wanted, prepared for, reared amid love and stability, and educated to the limit of their ability will mean more for the future of the black and brown races from which they come than any number of neglected, hungry, ill-housed and ill-clothed youngsters. Pride in one's race, as well as simple humanity, supports this view. Poor women of every race feel as I do, I believe. . . . It is the fear of such a future [poverty] that drives many women, of every color and social stratum, except perhaps the highest, to seek abortions when contraception has failed.[9]

Encouraged by the largest volume of mail her office had ever received in support of her position on an issue, Chisholm began planning an abortion repeal bill. Looking for House members, both conservative and liberal from both parties, who might support her bill, Chisholm wrote letters to a number of highly influential House members. Her strategy of adding conservative Republicans and Democrats as co-sponsors, together with the usual group of liberal Democrats, was eminently sound but failed to garner support. Some members said that they would vote for the bill if it ever reached the floor but could not support it publicly before then or work for its passage. Others expressed sympathy if not in agreement and still others rejected her bill as "trouble they didn't need." The bill languished in a drawer while Chisholm's approach shifted to organizing and galvanizing the overwhelming public support for the freedom to choose a safe, legal abortion.

The development and implementation of human service programs for women, minorities, and the poor are hallmarks of Chisholm's legislative tenure. But she also fought hard for the equitable administration of existing laws for all disenfranchised and marginated groups. In 1971 Chisholm was appointed to the House Education and Labor Committee. During her six-year tenure on this committee, there were several policy fights on behalf of working-class whites, minorities, and women. The first major policy confrontation concerned the basic right of the entire U.S. population to quality education. In the ninety-sixth session of Congress, Chisholm introduced and cosponsored many bills designed to increase educational opportunities for poor white and minority youth. In addition, these bills were part of her attempts to increase minority female and working-class access to professional and graduate schools and to provide more opportunities for adult education and training in local communities.

Another successful arena of policy confrontation was the Haitian refugee crisis. Foreign-born blacks were blatantly discriminated against in their efforts to gain asylum from political oppression when compared to the increased asylum assistance for Latin American, Asian, and Middle Eastern refugees. The denial of moral and material assistance to Haitian refugees, many of whom perished at sea after being turned away by the United States, moved Chisholm to mobilize public opinion on behalf of these oppressed people. As chair of the Congressional Black Caucus Task Force on Haitian Refugees in May 1979, Chisholm issued a statement that called for more equitable and just processing of requests for Haitian resettlement in the United States. Shirley Chisholm used her seniority and political clout to start a congressional reassessment of U.S. relations with Haiti.

By far the most outstanding achievement in Shirley Chisholm's political career was her candidacy for president in 1971 as the first viable female presidential candidate of color. Her candidacy opened a door for women and minorities by serving as a catalyst for aggressive political action, and exposed the racism and sexism of many so-called liberal Democrats.

A 1972 *New York Times Magazine* article by Stephan Lesher described the presidential hopefuls John Lindsay and Senator George McGovern as

> scared that Shirley Chisholm and black voters would gang up to blunt their drives for the Democratic nomination.
>
> But it was not to be. The lofty dream of black politicians—to overcome their own personal prejudices and ambitions, and coalesce into a powerful force in Presidential politics—proved illusory. The painful truth is that in 1972, Presidential candidates either are taking the black vote for granted or, worse, they just don't give a damn. . . . George Wallace obviously neither wanted nor expected blacks to help him. Senator Edmund Muskie, early in his days as the Democratic front-runner, declared he would not take a Negro as a running mate. Senator George McGovern blazed through the primaries despite only scattered Negro support plus some late-blooming endorsements from black leaders. And Hubert Humphrey, who jawed his way through the early primaries echoing George Wallace on the busing and welfare issues, received the lion's share of black votes nonetheless.[10]
>
> At first, [Chisholm's] black brothers in Congress merely ignored her candidacy. Asked about Mrs. Chisholm's budding candidacy, U.S. Representative Louis Stokes of Ohio, Carl's brother, shrugged and laughed while Congressman Clay answered, "Who's Shirley Chisholm?". . .

Chisholm ... leapfrogged over the black politicians and unilaterally cornered the market on black Presidential aspirations. The other leaders were embarrassed into sullen silence. "They were standing around, peeing on their shoes," snapped a Chisholm aide, "so Shirley said the hell with it and got a campaign going. If she hadn't, we'd still be without a black candidate".[11]

Congressman Ronald Dellums of California was her only black supporter among her colleagues early in the race. Georgia State Representative Julian Bond had proposed that local black leaders should run in their own state primaries to provide local political power bases for blacks. His goal was to make the Democratic party come to terms with black political demands. By entering the race, Chisholm made the stratagem of running a black local son impossible. Georgia State Senator Leroy Johnson gave his formidable black organization in Atlanta to Muskie, Louis Stokes sided with Humphrey, and Alcee Hastings, a black Fort Lauderdale lawyer, jumped to Muskie. Chisholm recognized that black leaders had more to gain for themselves if they backed a winner, rather than forming a strong but faceless coalition for a black candidate. She described black male antipathy for her campaign as simple male chauvinism, saying that "Black male politicians were no different than white male politicians. . . . This 'woman thing' is so deep. I've found it out in this campaign if I never knew it before."[12]

Chisholm's campaign was underfinanced and lacked effective organization. She often was unable to draw a crowd even in black neighborhoods and exhorted both blacks and whites to take her candidacy seriously. When her organization was able to produce crowds, she was able to galvanize whites and blacks alike from all social strata to her cause.

In analyzing her campaign, Chisholm concluded that for blacks to advance in the political arena, black politicians must accept their blackness and form an ideological base from which to operate. She declared that to be elected where the electorate is not solidly black, blacks must stay aware of the six points Julian Bond outlined in the second issue of *The Black Politician*:

1. Social, economic, education, political and physical segregation and discrimination fill a very real need for the white majority.

2. Appeals to justice and fair play are outmoded and useless when power, financial gain and prestige are at stake.

3. Positions of segregation and discrimination will be adhered to until change is forced through coercion, threats, power or violence.

4. Initiative for black political organization and education must come from within the Negro community and must be sustained on a day-to-day basis.

5. The geographical distribution of Negroes makes Negro-white coalitions desirable, but only when based on racial self-interest and genuine equality between the coalescing groups.

6. Racial self-interest, race consciousness and racial solidarity must always be paramount in the words and deeds of blacks in politics; when self-interest is forgotten, organized racism will continue to dominate and frustrate the best-organized actions of any black political unit, and leave it powerless and defenseless.[13]

Throughout Chisholm's campaign, the importance of strong coalition building was obvious. (Indeed, the later failure of the Ferraro bid for the vice presidency can be traced to the inability of the Mondale/Ferraro ticket to build effective coalitions among white males, white females, and people of color.) Progressive whites, minorities, and women cannot successfully manipulate the political machines that control presidential elections without strong coalition building, and the failure of women's groups to closely align their goals with racial minorities will result in continued exclusion of both groups from economic, foreign, and social policymaking circles.

Women in politics must understand more than coalition building to succeed. Women in politics must develop an intuitive and theoretical understanding of the policymaking process. Because women and minorities have been excluded from this process they often fail to understand "how" and "when" crucial decisions are made. In Chisholm's early political career, many decisions and policies in the Brooklyn Democratic Club were made in secret and numerous attempts were made to exclude her voice from the policymaking process in the Democratic party and in the Congress. This issue cannot be overstated: Women in politics must affect existing governmental institutions while they simultaneously create new political processes and progressive policies.

In many cases, the effectiveness of women in politics depends on their ability to gain the respect of political adversaries and Chisholm's ability to garner the support of ideological adversaries for individual issues was a positive characteristic of her political career. Although Chisholm initially faced harsh criticism for aligning herself with opponents on specific party issues, this practice has gained acceptance in recent years. Chisholm's ability to form friendships and positive relationships with political opponents, such as George Wallace, helped ensure passage of a bill she supported on behalf of domestic enablers.

Future female politicians will find Chisholm's political style a useful model for effecting coalition building within and across political parties in order to develop and implement policies.

Forging New Frontiers for Women

Chisholm's ascent to a position of power and respect in a male-dominated and male-controlled profession was far from easy. Chisholm often states, to the displeasure of many black males, that sexism was by far the strongest barrier to her success. Her espousal of feminism aroused the ire of both black men and women because many minority communities see the feminist movement as synonymous with white middle-class female privilege. As white women have traditionally benefited from racism and have failed to effectively challenge inequities facing women of color inside the feminist community and within the larger society, many white feminist leaders did not support Chisholm's bid for the presidency. In spite of the lack of support of both black males and white females for her quest for the presidency, her commitment to equal opportunity for both blacks and women has remained constant. Chisholm pioneered the notion of human-centered coalitions as opposed to women-centered or white or black male-centered coalitions as the rule for effective political action.

Shirley Chisholm's record on women's issues is outstanding. In addition to pushing for education and training legislation, she was among the first to fight for minimum wage policies to help domestic workers, who are primarily female, poor, and single heads of households. Chisholm has worked hard to promote the careers of women of all colors and has encouraged them to enter politics at the highest levels. She has used her power and influence to speak out on defense policies and human rights issues that lack feminine perspective.

In the mid-1980s, racist and sexist barriers still exist in the U.S. political system. During a telephone interview, Chisholm noted that black females in politics face a harder battle than their white counterparts. In fact Chisholm stated that many political pundits acknowledge that she is highly qualified for top political and governmental positions, and attribute her lack of recognition to her blackness. In essence, the barriers of sexism in political life have been bridged to a great extent by Chisholm, but racism still poses a threat to presidential hopefuls.

In response to this perception, many female activists and policymakers who also happen to be black are forming their own coalitions and associations. The most dynamic of these organizations is the National Black Women's Political Caucus, which was started by Shirley Chisholm. To some the formation of these associations confirms the exclusion of black women from existing organizations, but the experiences of Shirley Chisholm and other black women in politics reinforce the need for these organizations as a complement to traditional women's associations.

Discouraged by a conservative mood in the country, Chisholm retired from Congress in 1982 in order to spend time with her husband of four years who had been seriously injured in a car accident. But Shirley Chisholm paved the way for female politicians by sensitizing the Democratic party and the U.S. political system to the dynamism and ethical leadership of women. She has symbolized change and progressive reform to the political system.

Through her ability to represent and communicate effectively with ethically and politically diverse people, her leadership ability, and intuitive knowledge of the policy process, Chisholm provides an excellent case study of women in the policymaking process.

Notes

1. Shirley Chisholm, *Unbought and Unbossed.* Houghton Mifflin & Co., Boston, 1970, 14.
2. Ibid., 14.
3. Ibid., 14.
4. Ibid., 9.
5. Ibid., 15–16.
6. Ibid., 96–97.
7. Ibid., 97.
8. Ibid., 111.
9. Ibid., 114–115.
10. Stephan Lesher, "The Short Unhappy Life of Black Presidential Politics, 1972" *N.Y. Times Magazine.* June 25, 1972, 12.
11. Ibid., 13.
12. Ibid., 19.
13. Shirley Chisholm, *Unbought and Unbossed,* 148.

Dianne Feinstein:
Now That Was a Mayor!

KIRSTEN AMUNDSEN

After nine years as city boss of dazzling and bewildering San Francisco, Dianne Feinstein is surely the most celebrated woman mayor in the United States. Forced into retirement by the City Charter in 1987, Madame Mayor, as her associates still call her, can point to an impressive record of accomplishments and a heady list of honors bestowed upon her from far and near. Her critics, too, are many and diverse. Yet they will agree with her far more numerous admirers on one thing: We haven't heard the last of Dianne Feinstein.

Indeed, it would be a shame if the hard-earned experience and finely honed skills of this attractive politician were not put to use in the public arena of the future. Judging from observations made during the last few years, it would be quite a surprise as well. For with the hurdles she has encountered, the knocks received, and the strains endured have come a confidence and mastery of politics that promise to take Dianne Feinstein very far, should she decide to go for it. Indications are strong that she may do just that.

An interesting column by Jon Carrol of the *San Francisco Chronicle* in March 1986 touched on the transformation Dianne Feinstein has undergone since her startling debut on the city political scene in 1970. Contemplating an old photograph in which the new and only female supervisor in San Francisco is surrounded by male power brokers, Carrol notes the "panic in her face, a slump in her shoulders... that fearful sideways glance at her colleagues and superiors." And he speculates, "What did it take her, in terms of courage and energy and shrewd native intelligence to get to be a big city boss? She beat them all—because of her fear or despite of it."[1]

21

A self-made woman, yes. But more: a reinvented woman, according to this San Francisco columnist. In twenty years, Carrol predicts, some older person will say to a younger person, "Ah, you shoulda been here when Feinstein was running things. Now that was a MAYOR!"

High praise that, from a breed of writers best known for amusing slights or stinging barbs vis-à-vis politicians. Dianne Feinstein has had her share of that, too, not the least from the city's most famous columnist. Herb Caen— Mr. San Francisco himself—in a recent description of Feinstein when she first entered politics, remarked that she was "very much a Jewish Princess housewife." He then added, "She *still* is."[2]

Yet any inquiry into the mayor's past as well as into her present life and preoccupations prove that Caen missed the point. Although Jewish and a wife for most of her adult life, Dianne Feinstein had little comfort or security in her childhood and youth. Nor did she during her three marriages display much love for or skill in housewifery, admitting laughingly that she "knows how to boil water." Instead, her strength, both personal and political, may derive more from the trials and pain imposed upon her during a very difficult childhood as well as from later encounters with the tragic, even extraordinarily shocking, deaths of persons dear or near to her. Her hard-won accomplishments in the sometimes bizarre political battleground of San Francisco surely have nothing to do with her matronly status, for which she earned far more derision than compliments during the many years spent as a public servant.

Feinstein's difficult childhood surely played a major part in forming that strength of character for which she is now known. Feinstein was materially secure, even privileged, but her mother suffered from a brain disorder caused by childhood encephalitis. It caused erratic, often very violent behavior and was not diagnosed until she reached middle age. Dianne's father, a surgeon and professor, did his best to shield Dianne and her two younger sisters, but their mother's unpredictable behavior left deep scars on the family, as Dianne herself has testified. Dedication, persistence, and plain hard work mark Feinstein's political career as well as that native intelligence and courage she had to draw on from the very start to propel herself in a new and challenging direction.

What Makes Feinstein Run?

Dianne Feinstein first came to national attention on the tragic day in November 1978 when she stepped in front of a stunned and grieving crowd to confirm the dreadful news that Mayor George Moscone and Supervisor Harvey Milk had just been shot dead in their offices in City Hall by Supervisor Dan White. As president of the Board of Supervisors and therefore acting mayor, it was Feinstein's duty to make this announcement. With blood still on her skirt (she had come straight from the offices of the slain men), her voice held steady while it reverberated under the incredible stress of the hour. To a city just confronted with a second trauma following the Jonestown massacre the week before—in which so many San Franciscans were involved (the site of the Reverend James Jones' Peoples Temple was in the city itself)—the words and demeanor of their new mayor managed to do the trick. She soothed and gave direction to the city and suggested hope in the midst of the horror. "As we reconstructed the city after the physical damage done by an earthquake and fire, so too can we rebuild from the spiritual damage."[3]

It was, everyone agreed, a most impressive debut for a new mayor in the most trying of circumstances. This time Dianne Feinstein was precisely the leader San Francisco needed. Her integrity and sensitivity, together with unsuspected strength under great pressure, presented a much needed antidote to the frenzy and rumored political corruption in this Bagdad by the Bay, as Herb Caen aptly names the city. The irony was that Dianne Feinstein twice had been rejected as a mayoral candidate by the very electorate that from here on gave her its overwhelming support. She had, in fact, considered resigning from politics after serving out her third term as supervisor until Dan White's vengeful double murder catapulted her into the position she had given up hope of attaining. Or so she later said.

Only forty-five years of age at the time she took up the mantle from charismatic, yet erratic Mayor Moscone, Dianne Feinstein already had behind her a political record impressive enough to make anyone doubt that she could or would just abdicate her political duties and opportunities. Her first run for public office was, in fact, in the early 1950s when she won the vice presidency of the heavily male Stanford student body. Graduating with a double degree in history and political science in 1955, she immediately sought and won a CORO Foundation public affairs fellowship and spent the following year specializing in criminal justice. Married briefly to a young district attorney in 1956, she bore her only child and was divorced before her daughter reached the age of one. In 1962 she was married again, this time to a man nineteen years her senior, neurosurgeon Bertraum Feinstein. It was by all accounts a happy and solid marriage; Dr. Feinstein gave Dianne support for whatever endeavors she wanted to undertake.

And what she wanted, it turned out, was politics. The lovely home in San Francisco's fashionable Pacific Heights and a close-knit family as well as an active cultural and social life could not for long satisfy the private yearnings and public aspirations of Dianne Feinstein. Her concern and expertise in the field of criminal justice involved her with several agencies, including the city's Advisory Committee for Adult Detention, which she chaired from 1967 to 1969. Her circle of friends and supporters grew measurably as her dedication and effectiveness in public service became known. In 1969 she made the decision to become a full-fledged politician. She ran for a seat on the Board of Supervisors—certainly a radical thing for a woman in her position to do at the time. She was in fact warned that San Francisco already had one woman supervisor and that there could be only one of those on the board! Dianne defied the opposition, however, and won the race with the greatest plurality earned by any candidate. That victory earned her by statute the presidency of the Board of Supervisors, the first woman ever elected to this position. Again, she paid no heed as old "pros" told her it would be "inappropriate" for a woman to be president of the board. From here on in Dianne Feinstein was a celebrity as well as a genuine power broker in "the city that knows how."

Yet only two years later she made what many consider a major political mistake. She decided to run for mayor against a popular, powerful, but reportedly corrupt incumbent, Joe Alioto. Running on a proenvironment and antismut platform, she was also an advocate for school integration. With her own daughter in private school, she was quickly labeled a hypocrite by skeptics in the media. In a city priding itself on its tolerance—even license—her stern attitude against the spread of nudie bars and fleshpots of all possible variety also earned her a whole new set of enemies. Her insecurity and lack of experience in this type of race also showed—as in the much talked about incident where a line of strippers doing the Can Can interrupted her press conference. Today Dianne's response would most likely be a hearty laugh—but in 1971 she became seriously unnerved. No sense of humor, said her critics, and yet another charge was added to shore up the image of "goody two shoes," the candidate with "white gloves," the "Pacific Heights matron" who would be mayor. All of that certainly didn't help her campaign. Dianne Feinstein resents these characterizations to this very day but can now afford to smile about them, however wryly. Her decision to run against Mayor Alioto was prompted by the conviction that somebody had to, that somebody with a chance for success must challenge this all too powerful and yet charming "machine" politician.

Despite the sound defeat she suffered, Dianne Feinstein was back on the Board of Supervisors in 1974 and decided to try again for mayor in 1975. Her opponent was the charismatic George Moscone, who had the wholehearted support both of labor unions and San Francisco's gay community, reported to number 100,000 in a city of 744,000. Mayoral elections in San Francisco are not party affairs, and the backing of a cohesive, well-organized bloc of voters is therefore of inestimable value in such contests. Dianne Feinstein was whipped again.

Her work as a supervisor was widely recognized, however, as evidenced by her three terms as president of the board. But in 1978 her loyal, loving husband died a slow and painful death of cancer. It was the second time

Dianne Feinstein had to deal with this agony; her father died of cancer in similar circumstances. Near emotional exhaustion and at this point very tired of leading the Board of Supervisors, Dianne Feinstein saw no future prospects for herself in city politics. In fact, she had decided to quit after the horror of the Jonestown massacre hit the news and deeply disturbed the many San Franciscans who knew or were involved with Pastor Jones and his followers at the People's Temple. Yet a greater horror lay in wait for the city. This one forced Dianne once more to reevaluate her commitments and turned out to change both her and the city's future.

A Perfectionist Mayor

From the moment she came upon the bloodied bodies of supervisor Harvey Milk and Mayor George Moscone in their offices in City Hall, Dianne Feinstein knew this was not the time to turn her back on city politics. Not only was it her duty to assume the position as acting mayor, she also had to find a way to bring to citizens devastated by this succession of traumatic events some solace, an intimation of hope through a rededication to the future of the city.

Rebuild, she said. And rebuild she did. As quickly as possible Dianne Feinstein took charge and infused a new spirit—with a new discipline—in the often chaotic politics of San Francisco's City Hall. While retaining most of former Mayor Moscone's staff, the style of administration was a different one. Dress codes, punctuality, and long working hours for the mayor and high-level appointees now came to be the order of the day. Effectiveness, integrity, and attention to detail were to be the hallmarks of Dianne Feinstein's stewardship of City Hall.

The first task at hand was to balance the city budget, seriously out of whack with a $127 million deficit the year she took office. Less than four years later it showed a $150 million surplus. Crime was another priority for the new mayor, and, again, she could soon point to significant improvements. San Francisco's crime rate showed a decline of 10 percent in 1982, following a similar decline the year before. Unemployment in San Francisco also was brought down in Dianne Feinstein's administration and has held steadily below state and national levels. With construction of new businesses at an all-time high in recent years, San Francisco can surely compete for the title of the most prosperous large city in the United States.

So thriving and attractive was San Francisco that in 1984 it was chosen as the site for the Democratic Presidential Convention—in spite of misgivings among some politicians about the city's image as the gay capital of the United States. Dianne Feinstein fought hard for the city to be given this honor. She also succeeded in the drive she spearheaded to renovate and repair the city's famed cable cars. It took two years and was exceedingly costly, but the massive celebration that greeted the return of the favored old hill-climbing vehicles in 1984 gave ample testimony to their significance and popularity among city dwellers and visitors both.

The Democratic Presidential Convention of 1984 also marked a new high in Dianne Feinstein's career. She emerged as a top contender for the candidacy for the vice presidency, one of the select few who met with Walter Mondale at his home in Minnesota prior to the San Francisco meetings. The presidential candidate himself was much impressed, as were all audiences and observers getting to know Dianne Feinstein on the occasion of her emergence to national prominence. Appearing on national television, both NBC's "Today" and CBS' "Morning News" as well as the "Phil Donahue Show," and then profiled by *Reader's Digest* and *People* magazines, the mayor both looked and sounded good enough to become a favored speaker for audiences across the nation, receiving far many more speaking requests than she could reasonably fill.

Dianne Feinstein's success as mayor of San Francisco is still the foundation of her national recognition and promise. Her great pride is the fiscal solvency, improved safety, and general livability of the city. San Francisco is a well-run city, she says herself, and that is clearly important in today's troubled urban scene. As a spokeswoman for the cities, Mayor Feinstein has lobbied frequently and effectively in Washington, D.C. Heading the U.S. Conference of Mayors, she strongly argued against reduction of aid for poor city dwellers before Congress in 1986.

Her crowning achievement may well be the downtown plan finalized in 1986, making San Francisco the first city in the nation to enact strong controls on the height and shape of buildings in the downtown core. The hills, parks, and the vistas of San Francisco, famous around the world, have for some time been threatened by the creeping Manhattanization of the central area. The downtown plan is an effort to control the big business boom in the city, to ensure that esthetic and environmental concerns are given due consideration. The plan also is accompanied by precedent-setting legislation providing for affordable child care, low-income housing, the preservation of 250 buildings of architectural merit, and requirements for art and open space.

Dianne Feinstein took the initiative and shepherded the downtown plan through its many and lengthy phases to its final successful form. It was an excruciatingly difficult process—a gnashing of teeth and endless compromises, in the words of supervisor Carol Ruth Silver. But it also puts San Francisco at the cutting edge of the urban renewal movement and promises to retain the city's special charm and livability as well as provide plentiful opportunities for the many businesses that want to settle or operate here.

The rebuilding of San Francisco's port, neglected for many years until

Mayor Feinstein took office, is another ambition now well on its way to fulfillment. New container terminals and transfer facilities are being built, new contracts are coming in, and revenues were up 22 percent in the spring of 1986. Mayor Feinstein sees ship repairs as a major source of blue-collar jobs. The chances for developing this vital revenue greatly improved when San Francisco was designated as the home port for the USS *Missouri*. With it came one cruiser, four frigates, two minesweepers, and an estimated four thousand new jobs created by demands for ship repairs, housing construction, and base improvements. Again, it was the mayor who spearheaded the movement to make San Francisco the home port of the USS *Missouri*. She had the help of some supervisors as well as U.S. Representative Barbara Boxer and Senator Pete Wilson. Yet her own lobbying in Washington for the homeport movement was, as in other cases, of great significance.

How does she do it? What is the key to her undoubted effectiveness as administrator, as lobbyist, and as bridge builder among the various branches of government, the business community, and citizens? Those who know her best point to her commitment to work and to performance on the job as well as to the hands-on approach and attention to details as her greatest assets in the never ending struggle to get things accomplished in a big bureaucracy. A highly capable administrator, she involves herself directly in every sphere of city government, sometimes to the despair of her hard-driven staff. She also is known for giving everyone an ear and often will try to bring together constituents with differing points of view. Consensus building has become one of her great fortes. Her unquestioned integrity no doubt stands her in excellent stead in any confrontation. Even her enemies have to admit that Dianne Feinstein is that rare species: a big city mayor untouched by even a breath of scandal!

To all of that can be added this: Dianne Feinstein has charm. It adds immeasurably to her persuasiveness, not the least in heavily male leadership circles. She is direct in her approach, yet can be very warm and, on occasion, surprisingly witty. The earlier insecurity observed by many as she first approached crowds has been replaced by confidence and genuine pleasure as she confronts new audiences. She can even work the crowd now, according to one of her staff members. And end up liking it! She has, in other words, become a consummate politician.

Balancing on the Tightrope

Even the greatest fan of San Francisco will admit that this is not exactly a city of civic harmony and moderation. It has, in fact, one of the most volatile ethnic and political make-ups imaginable in the United States today. The city is polarized between richly diverse ethnic groups, each with different and frequently competing claims on city government. The conflict between the "downtown" business interests and environmentalists is intense at times; the claims of the city's lower-income sector can clash with either group.

Organized labor is also very strong in San Francisco, so strong that the unions have won wage settlements that put the city at the top of the scale of union wages nationwide. Mayor Feinstein was, in fact, informed by the Department of Housing and Urban Development in 1986 that the agency no longer will tolerate any craft wages beyond prevailing rates. This, said the mayor in an almost classic understatement, presents very real problems with certain unions.

Then there is San Francisco's massive gay population to reckon with. The liberal character of the city and its famed tolerance have attracted more than 100,000 homosexuals and lesbians at this time. Using gay voting power, or the threat of it, they have won for themselves more rights and privileges in this Mecca of gays than anywhere else in the nation—or the world. They have, of course, contributed to making San Francisco the first city in the nation where more than half the population is made up of nonfamily households. The city scene is increasingly dominated by "yuppies," both gays and straights. That fact, together with what is called the "restaurant sprawl" (San Francisco has the highest number of restaurants per capita in the nation), is a constant source of irritation and concern for families in the old neighborhoods. Housing costs have shot up alarmingly to the point where people on lower or average incomes feel themselves virtually squeezed out of the city.

All of them, every single faction, organization, or irate individual, take their problems and claims to City Hall where they very often are put squarely in Dianne Feinstein's lap. It is a political tightrope that is not easily navigated. It is also what makes city politics an art, according to the mayor. To some of those closest to her, both politically and personally, her greatest achievement is simply holding the city together, in the words of supervisor Louise Renne. To her old friend and backer Morris Bernstein, Dianne Feinstein must be credited first of all with "keeping the city cool." In a place like San Francisco, where it is "a way of life to dispute anything," that alone is a great accomplishment.

Yet Dianne Feinstein has surely had her share of missteps; she has come very close at times to falling off the tightrope. In 1983 she had to face an agonizing and costly recall campaign, launched by a motley group of opponents, led by the radical right wing White Panthers. What made them mad was Feinstein's strong support of a handgun-control bill passed by the Board of Supervisors, making San Francisco the first major city with such an ordinance. This tiny group of activists was joined by voters in the homosexual community, angry because the mayor dared to veto a bill that would have given gays and other singles living together the same joint insurance benefits received by married couples. Together with other disgruntled citizens in the city, these groups managed to gather enough signatures on the petition for a recall election. It was a humiliating experience for Dianne Feinstein and yet another chance for her to show her mettle. She threw herself into the fight, working the streets and the crowds like never before. And she won, with an impressive 82 percent of the vote.

Her critics remain, of course, and they most often charge her with being too close to the "downtown interests." She has allowed San Francisco to become a tourist city, she is much too friendly with the developers and financiers, she has not appointed enough minority members to commissions, and she refuses to extend rent control to newly vacated housing.

Dianne Feinstein has answers to the whole litany of complaints. She does support rent control, for instance, but to extend it as proposed would make builders reject new construction. She strongly defends her own record here, claiming it is the very attractiveness of the city that has caused the dramatic rise in the cost of housing. As to the charge of allowing big business to march in and take over the city, she reminds her critics that she is the mayor of the entire city, which includes the business community. Dianne Feinstein rather prides herself on having presided over the growth that has made San Francisco's economy one of the most robust in the nation while supporting the new downtown plan, the toughest one in the nation in terms of controlling the height and shape of business buildings in the core area.

The mayor's balancing act is what really irks some of her constituents. She is very much a centrist in her political views generally, altogether too staid according to certain critics. A lifelong Democrat, she was an early backer of both Jimmy Carter and Walter Mondale, but she has nevertheless taken foreign policy positions closer to President Reagan than to the left wing of the Democratic party. Thus, she came out in support of the U.S. bombing raid on Libya in April 1986 and is known to favor a strong defense for the United States.

Dianne Feinstein indeed is recognized for her ability to work very well with the private sector. Again and again she has turned to this sector for aid in dealing with some of the city's critical financial problems—and has received most of what she needed. Early in her administration a high-powered brain trust called the Mayor's Fiscal Advisory Committee was set up, consisting of thirty-five corporate and business leaders. It is reported to have saved the city multimillions of dollars and has set up managerial training policies that are among the most effective and progressive anywhere in the nation.

Her new life partner also comes from this group. In 1980 Dianne Feinstein married Richard Blum, a financier and outdoor adventurer who chaired the committee. He provides her with a special input from the financial community and is also a Democrat and a friend of former President Jimmy Carter. The mayor and her husband are known to lead very active independent lives in a union that allows for this autonomy and for the closeness and mutual support needed by people in public life. Dianne Feinstein and Richard Blum may have formed the ultimate public-private partnership, in the comment of columnist Neil Peirce.[4] Fittingly enough, the wedding ceremony took place in San Francisco's beautiful City Hall—with five thousand people joining the party.

Women's Issues

In 1984 Dianne Feinstein was one of the favorites of Democratic women pushing for a woman to be the party's vice presidential candidate. She was—and still is—celebrated as a perfect role model for the successful female politician in the 1980s. Yet she is not known as an ardent feminist, and women's issues have not been at the top of her agenda at any time during her eighteen years as a politician. It would be difficult for anyone to accuse—or laud—her for being a banner carrier for women.

Dianne Feinstein is, of course, in support of the Equal Rights Amendment and frequently lobbied for its passage before its defeat in 1984. Yet she refused to have traveling members of her staff join a city boycott of states that had not ratified the ERA, finding such action counterproductive. She also is supportive of women's right to choose abortion but has not been in the forefront on this issue. As to child care, Mayor Feinstein is strongly concerned with fulfilling this compelling need in her city. Due largely to her initiative, new funds are being channelled into child care facilities in San Francisco. The Downtown Plan specifically incorporates an Affordable Child Care Fund, another precedent-setting move taken by the mayor.

On one significant feminist issue, comparative worth—a bottom line issue, according to activists—Dianne Feinstein came at loggerheads with the feminist movement in the city. The majority of supervisors gave support to a plan that called for, among other things, a meal allowance of $5.00 daily for city workers earning less than $26,000 per year. The scheme, termed "ill-advised" by the mayor, would total $28 million, with Social Security and retirement benefits potentially adding another $2 million yearly to the city budget. Dianne Feinstein vetoed the plan. Fiscal responsibility and the questionable legality of the supervisors' initiative were the key issues. Comparative worth is a state and not a local issue, said Feinstein. For many feminists in the city, however, this was proof that Dianne Feinstein was not one of them, that she was an "outsider" to the movement, as one of them put it. Voters vindicated the mayor's stand when the plan was put on the ballot as Proposition E in 1985 and was defeated by 80 percent.

Dianne Feinstein also is fully aware that in some of her past campaigns, women did not vote for her. In 1975 the National Organization for Women, in fact, endorsed George Moscone for mayor when Dianne was one of his prime contenders. It hurt, seeing the rejection in women's faces, she says. Now women tend to be proud of women in politics, and Dianne Feinstein confirms that she has recently run better among women than among men.

All of this fits quite neatly with Mayor Feinstein's image as a center politician, frustrating activists both on the left and the right with her cool moderation. Yet Dianne Feinstein also has been very supportive of women politicians and has sought out capable women from many fields to fill vacancies created in city government. She has done a super job for women, according to Supervisor Louise Renne, who has accompanied the mayor on several of her trips abroad.

Supervisor Renne also puts her finger on one of Dianne Feinstein's greatest, if inadvertent, contributions to the women's cause: her very visibility as leader in a field so overwhelmingly occupied by men. She is noticed more, she catches attention, and—with both her reputation, her command of issues, and her undoubted charm—she awakens both women and men to the possibility and desirability of bringing women into political life on the highest level. Louise Renne recalls that when she accompanied the mayor on her first trip to China, they did not meet with a single woman decisionmaker. Yet when a Chinese delegation came on a reciprocal visit to San Francisco to formalize the sister-city relationship established with Shanghai, several women were included.

Dianne Feinstein is keenly aware of her potential contribution as a role model for aspiring young women politicians. She doesn't mince words about the difficulties facing them and herself. The pressure to be tough, for instance, presents a double bind for women in executive positions. There is on the one hand the fear that women can't be strong enough. Then, if they prove themselves to be, they are labeled "iron maidens." Yet she finds hope in the "natural evolution" taking place, with more women moving into all aspects of the business world and professions, and she stresses the value of networking among women.

In a commencement address at Mills College for women, the mayor gave very direct advice on how best to succeed. "First, women should know that breaking out of the mold is not easy. Cracking into traditional male positions requires more than a good education. It requires character, strong motivation, and plain hard work." As to the secret for success, she advises:

> Become an expert. We women—so eager to participate—have a tendency to spread ourselves too thin. . . . A better way is to carefully select an area—one area—to focus on. Then really bore in. Read everything you can find on the subject. Talk with the achievers in the field. . . . Join the appropriate organizations. . . . Get involved for the long, not the short term. . . . Become publicly identified with your chosen field. You will become a factor for change, and you will also find yourself in demand.

Mayor Feinstein's words in this case appear to describe her own chosen path to public office. And it is hard to argue with success.

Feinstein's Future

What is ahead for Dianne Feinstein as she steps down from her mayoral post in 1987? The comfortable, even plush retirement that awaits her should she now choose to be both Mrs. Richard Blum and the honorable ex-mayor of San Francisco is the least likely path of any for her to take, friends and associates agree. Yet as one casts about for opportunities lying ahead for this seasoned and talented politician, it is clear that her fortunes are pretty much tied to the Democratic party. A Democratic victory in the presidential election of 1988 will put her in immediate reach of high national office—a cabinet post or an important international assignment. Barring that, she will have to await the electoral openings that may appear on state and national levels.

Mayor Feinstein could, of course, have chosen to contend with Senator Alan Cranston and Mayor Tom Bradley in the Democratic primary in 1986 for—respectively—the senatorial or the gubernatorial nomination. Both were considered within her reach and on her agenda of political aspirations. Yet she refrained from that challenge because of loyalty and promises made in the case of Bradley and concern for party unity in the case of Cranston.

Some say that what Dianne Feinstein really wants is to be president of the United States. In an interview with Tom Horton in 1984 she spoke frankly about that ambition. "I would like to go on, yes," she said, "in major national office. The presidency or vice presidency." She was on the road when she said it, Horton points out. In a review written of Susan J. Carroll's "Women as Candidates in American Politics," Dianne Feinstein agreed with enthusiasm that in the future more and more women will be important in politics. It will happen, in her analysis, as they "exploit their electoral successes and realize still greater ambitions by running for and capturing higher and higher office."[5]

Yet another clue to Dianne Feinstein's future may be in a newfound role greatly savored by the mayor. As San Francisco's ambassador to the world, she has exhibited impressive skills and winning charm as a diplomat. Her first trip abroad as mayor in 1979 was to China. It turned out a stunning success. A sister-city relationship was established with Shanghai, which included the first Chinese Consulate in the United States, regular air service, Chinese shipping contracts for the San Francisco port, and fifty-five other cultural and economic projects. It is, says Dianne Feinstein, the most active sister-city program anywhere.

The mayor's travels abroad became more frequent as her administration came to an end. No less than nine sister-city relationship had been established by 1987. The year before Dianne Feinstein went on two of her most interesting and challenging trips—to the Soviet Union and to Israel. She met with Mikhail Gorbachev, lobbied—successfully in at least one case—for the release of Soviet Jews wishing to emigrate, and negotiated agreements for exchanges of symphony, art, ballet, and opera, particularly between San Francisco and what she hoped to be one more sister city: Leningrad. That plan was thwarted, at least temporarily, by opposition from some members of San Francisco's Jewish community and in the state legislature by Art Agnos, Democratic member from San Francisco.

Just a few months after this trip, Mayor Feinstein went on a whirlwind tour of Israel, on the occasion of signing a shipping agreement between ZIM (the Israeli state shipping agency) and the port of San Francisco. Again, she made maximum use of her opportunity, not just to arrange another sister-city relationship—this time with Haifa—but to meet with Israeli leaders and to even work the crowds in Haifa. Eager to become an expert, she boned up on the politics of the Middle East, reading State Department briefings before getting the firsthand exposure to Israel's volatile political scene. She even took her first cautious step into Mideast politics here, according to Marshall Kilduff, a reporter accompanying her on this trip by coming out publicly in favor of a Palestinian homeland, if such a plan were backed by Arab countries and Israel.

"This is exciting," declared the Mayor. "I love it, love it, love it!"[6]

Indications are that both leaders and citizens abroad took to Dianne Feinstein as easily as she to them. In 1984 she was given the French Legion d'Honeur by President Francois Mitterand. It is a much treasured award for the mayor who prides herself on having led San Francisco in an international renaissance. Dianne Feinstein strongly believes in the potential of the Pacific Rim. She herself has done a great deal to exploit the opportunities opening up abroad for San Francisco. And that, in the end, may point the way to new and greater opportunities for Dianne Feinstein.

Notes

1. *San Francisco Chronicle,* March 11, 1986, 63.

2. *San Francisco Focus Magazine* (April 1986):95.

3. Quoted in article by Cynthia Gorney, "Mayor Dianne Feinstein—Gaining Clout," *Washington Post,* July 25, 1984, sec. B.

4. Neil Peirce, *San Francisco Examiner,* June 6, 1982, 88.

5. Quoted in the *San Francisco Chronicle,* August 8, 1985, 65.

6. *San Francisco Chronicle,* March 8, 1986, 5.

Congresswoman Geraldine A. Ferraro: An American Legacy

ARTHUR J. HUGHES and FRANK P. Le VENESS

Geraldine A. Ferraro, first woman vice presidential candidate in the history of this nation, represented the Ninth Congressional District in Queens County, New York, during three congresses, 1979–1985. During those years, she earned great esteem from her party for her loyalty and held the respect of her constituents for her work on their behalf.

Formative Years

Born on August 20, 1935, Ferraro was one of four children, two of whom survived, born to Antonetta Corrieri and Dominick Ferraro. Her mother was born in Manhattan to southern Italian immigrant parents; her father came from Southern Italy as a young man in his twenties. The family operated restaurants in Queens County (one of the five boroughs of New York City) and in Newburgh, New York. Her upbringing, and that of her older brother Carl, was conventional and comfortable, surrounded by the security of loving parents and the knowledge that an extended family of cousins, aunts, uncles, and grandparents provided support and encouragement.

A precocious child, Gerry Ferraro was a quick learner, with a deep curiosity about the world around her. She never crawled as a baby—she walked, and her pace has not abated since. During her college days her grandmother, watching Geraldine race through the morning dressing routine, remarked, "Everybody gets dressed in 1-2-3 except Gerry. She gets dressed in 1."[1]

Life for the Ferraros changed drastically when Dominick died of a heart attack in 1944, leaving his widow with a teenage son and eight-year-old Geraldine to raise. Shattered by grief, Antonetta heeded too much advice too quickly—she sold the Newburgh assets and moved to the Bronx. She returned to her early craft of crochet beading and used her earnings to send her son Carl through military school and to permit Geraldine to become a boarder at Marymount School.

Geraldine received much of her elementary school education and all of high school at Marymount. After graduation from high school, she was offered a tuition scholarship to Marymount College, a stroke of good fortune that today would be greeted with universal celebration among friends and family. Not so in the Italian-America of 1952. What did a healthy, pretty, sixteen-year-old girl need of a college education? "Who goes to college anyway," asked her relatives, "when there are plenty of jobs around for clerks and secretaries?" In this way, some of Geraldine's older male relatives sniffed at her college pretensions, and she was at a disadvantage without a father's encouragement. But here Antonetta filled the place of both parents, courageously urging her daughter on to a better life than she had had. Geraldine's decision to go on to college placed her on an equal par with her brother Carl, who was at Villanova, and her cousins, including Nicholas, who became an important part of her life as a public figure.

Without doubt, the two most important influences on her life were her religion and her mother. Geraldine was brought up in an environment of saints and sacraments, living much of her life by the sacred seasons of the liturgical year.

Religion is vital to Geraldine Ferraro today, a factor that may unconsciously account for her deep respect for former President Jimmy Carter. She calls her born-again political ally "a truly moral man." In her public life, the influences of both her religion and her mother seem evident throughout the various phases of her public career. For example, her determination to relieve the plight of the abused victims who sought her assistance while she headed the Abused Victims' Bureau of the Queens County District Attorney's office, or her fight in Congress for the rights of the poor, the oppressed, and those in need of social assistance.

In 1956, at the age of twenty, she graduated from Marymount and embarked on a teaching career. She was assigned to Public School 65 in Astoria, Queens. Ferraro threw herself enthusiastically into the education of New York City's youth and specialized in reading instruction. Without breaking stride, she entered Fordham University's School of Law and began a four-year night school grind toward embarking upon a legal career. While in college, she met John Zaccaro, himself a law student. They dated during the next few years and married within weeks after her graduation from Fordham in 1960.

By 1974, when her three children were old enough to permit her to work outside the home, she began casting about for a way to put her legal education to use. Her cousin, then District Attorney (D.A.) Nicholas Ferraro, in spite of a concern that he might be accused of nepotism, offered her a post as an assistant district attorney (A.D.A.) for Queens County. When asked why she joined the D.A.'s office, she replied candidly, "Because I wanted to go back to work full-time and it was the one place I knew I could get a job that was close to home, and because my cousin was the District Attorney." There was no question about her qualifications.

At thirty-eight, Geraldine Ferraro was no amateur. A solid, if modest, private practice had kept her hand at the law, and her life experience gave her many insights. Still, it was difficult for her: "Getting back into the practice of law after you're off for fourteen years is not easy," she recalled. "I understand the plight of the displaced homemaker like nobody does."

She did her job tenaciously, skillfully, heedless of time, and she won the respect of her peers. When her cousin Nicholas became a New York State Supreme Court judge, he was replaced as district attorney by John Santucci. Santucci decided to promote Gerry, and in mid-1977 she became head of a new unit, the Special Victim's Bureau. Her special qualifications as homemaker and mother had made her a person of compassion who could appreciate the trauma of an abused child.

When Geraldine Ferraro became bureau chief, she molded that bureau to fit the special needs of the clientele she served. She and her assistants became advocates for abused children as much as representatives of the state. It was a small bureau, with three or four lawyers and one investigator, but it achieved its goal—blazing a trail for future care of the helpless.

"Did you ever find being a woman was particularly helpful to you?" she was asked. "Sure," she answered frankly. "Would I have gotten to be Bureau Chief after four years in the D.A.'s office if I weren't a woman? I would like to say, that, yes, I would have gotten it because of my brains and personality and all that business, but honestly? I doubt it. I really doubt it."

In late 1977 she decided to leave the Queens D.A.'s office, but John Santucci convinced her to stay on a while longer. It is not hard to see why. She was good at what she did, throwing herself wholeheartedly into it. Her conviction record was a splendid one—in nineteen out of twenty cases she won for the people.

Congressional Election

Early in 1978, Ferraro decided to challenge Congressman James J. Delaney in the primary for the Democratic nomination in the Ninth Congressional District (C.D.). This was brave because "Delaney of the 9th" would be no pushover. To knowledgeable New Yorkers, the possibility conjured up images of Elizabeth Holtzman's successful overthrow of Emanuel Celler in Brooklyn a few years earlier. However, a Delaney-Ferraro contest would be complicated by the fact that the Queens County Democratic organization wanted City Councilman Thomas Manton to succeed Delaney. Manton had the county party chairman's blessing and was well liked by the district leaders of the Ninth C.D.

The Ninth Congressional District is composed of decent hard-working people who typically live in single-family frame houses. In 1978 it consisted of nine state assembly districts (A.D.s) in whole or part and about three hundred election districts (E.D.s). The A.D.s and the E.D.s are the infrastructure of every C.D., and at this level we come very realistically to grips with territoriality. An E.D. is a geographically compact division of an A.D. It may have as many as 800 persons, and along with other E.D.s forms the A.D., with an approximate population, in Queens, of 120,000. The C.D. encompasses 500,000 people. To win nomination, a Democrat must win the hearts of the A.D. leaders. Each of the nine assembly districts has two parts, and each part has a male and female leader. Thus, to win nomination, Geraldine Ferraro had to influence thirty-six tough political pragmatists.

There were many imponderables facing her as she took up the question of running for Congress in 1978. The family was called upon for input, and all members gave wholehearted support to the decision, including Antonetta, who responded with an enthusiastic "terrific." Almost before the primary campaign began the Ferraro camp learned of seventy-seven-year-old Congressman Delaney's decision to retire. The race was wide open, but not for long. At a spring meeting of district leaders, Ferraro won a disappointing two votes out of thirty-six. Because primaries are party elections, failure to gain leadership support is more often than not the kiss of death. Such a failure means no financial assistance and no organizational support; in ordinary circumstances it means defeat.

In Ferraro's case, money was not the impediment it is in many campaigns of this sort. During the years her husband's real estate business, built on foundations laid by his father, had prospered. The Zaccaros were very comfortable, and sources of money—contributions, loans, and family expenditures—were available to get the campaign started. But running a political campaign is much like staging a wedding—one thing leads to another. With printing costs, rent, gasoline, advertising, and a hundred other expenses, the money flowed out in undreamed-of quantities. By the time both primary and general elections were over, Geraldine Ferraro had spent a reported $382,074 compared with a combined $134,425 for her Republican and Democratic opponents. These figures and the source of her funds became significant factors in the summer of 1984 after her nomination as Walter Mondale's vice presidential running mate.[2]

In May she kicked off her campaign in what would become characteristic of her style. On the steps of New York's City Hall she publicly announced for the office, promising to restore industry in the district, protect the homeowner and tenant, revive the neighborhoods, and make certain that her future constituents would get "every penny" they "have coming to them" from the federal government. As a grass-roots campaigner, she was at her best when engaged in a frank, freewheeling exchange with constituents. They talked back to her, and she returned the compliment with spirit and occasional fire. "The American voters should be as involved with me as I am with them," she once remarked.

While Ferraro was campaigning, a staff of dedicated volunteers, including Antonetta Ferraro, was hard at work. They compiled the prime voting list, which listed potential voters in the district coded according to age, sex, ethnicity, party, and voting frequency. For six weeks, a team of earnest workers labored five days a week to collect the data, and none was as enthusiastic as Antonetta nor worked as hard. She was an inspiration, an aide recalled, and "always a delight" to be around. The list became the basis for four primary mailings to Democratic households. Meanwhile, fifteen hundred *valid* signatures were needed from registered Democrats in the district; many who had signed for her opponents did not wish to become involved or were unavailable.

The enthusiasm generated by Ferraro and her family was infectious. Volunteers were on the telephones for hours at night, bringing messages to voters. In the absence of newspapers—there were strikes against both the New York *Daily News* and *The New York Times* that summer—radio spots were used, and leaflets were distributed in great quantities. The entire operation was spectacularly professional.

Concerning the issues of the primary, less can be said. All three candidates were Catholics in a heavily Catholic district. All three were identifiably ethnic, and all were attractive, articulate, and knowledgeable. On most matters all three candidates agreed—except for abortion, which Ferraro described as "the worst issue" in the campaign.

She had wrestled with the question of abortion for years, and although she found it personally and morally repugnant, Ferraro could not find it in her conscience to advocate a public policy that forbade abortion to others. On this one issue, the Roman Catholic church and Ferraro parted company. Questions at church gatherings were strident, and minds were made up on this issue alone, but Ferraro held her own, retaining loyalty to her conscience and her church.

Her other stands marked her as a conservative, or at least a moderate Democrat with decided middle-class leanings. Her campaign fliers headlined the mottoes "Finally . . . a tough, independent Democrat" and "The middle-class way of life must be protected." Crime was a paramount issue in her campaign, as might be expected from a former A.D.A. Her strength in this area no doubt compensated for losses on the abortion issue, as did her stands on restoration of the death penalty, crackdowns on welfare cheats, treatment of juvenile offenders as adults in selected cases, and tuition tax credits for parochial and private schools, up to and including college.

The September primary ended the first phase of Ferraro's campaign for James Delaney's seat. Ferraro emerged victorious, winning 53 percent of the votes. After thanking her supporters profusely, the nominee went to county party headquarters for the traditional congratulations. Regardless of her position before, she was the anointed party candidate now. The following morning, without missing a beat, she was off to do battle with the Republican candidate, four-term assemblyman Alfred Dellibovi, who, not faced with a primary, was fresh and spoiling for a fight.

At thirty-two, he was one of the youngest politicians in the Republican camp and very influential. Al was political through and through; he played hardball and was enthusiastic and energetic. He studied his opponent well, seeking out every chink in her armor. The pace accelerated; the charges flew. Except for abortion, very few issues separated the candidates. The difference was that Dellibovi had a record in Albany, the state capital, to point to, while Ferraro could only promise. It came down to personality, money, hard work, tactics, and luck. "Thank God my first election was never reduced to issues," the congresswoman said. Had it been waged so, it is possible that Dellibovi might have won.

Instead, it became partly a media event and partly a case of charges thrown by each side against the other. The Carter White House decided Ferraro was a "comer" and brought out the heavy artillery, beginning with a late September meeting with the President. This was followed by a visit from the President's mother, who was returning from Pope John Paul I's funeral in Rome. The White House followed this up with several more salvos as the secretaries of labor and of health, education, and welfare visited the scene.

Dellibovi was just as energetic in his campaigning. A skillful debater, he met Ferraro several times in well-attended debates, but the arguments centered on personalities and charges more than on the issues. Dellibovi lashed out at the Ferraro campaign's heavy spending, because it could not be matched, demanding to know the sources of funding. "She has inexhaustible funds," one of the assemblyman's loyalists later remarked. "You knocked out one tank and another appeared." But, the commentator continued, she was "really superb the way she moved around, covering the bases."[3]

On election day November 1978, results in the Ninth C.D. were decisive. Geraldine Ferraro won 55 percent of the vote, thus becoming the first woman in the history of Queens County to win election to Congress. There were other aspects of her election that inevitably caused comment. Geraldine Ferraro was not identifiable as a feminist. Her campaign was run more on ethnic than on gender grounds, and her election made her the second Italian-American woman to serve in Congress, following Connecticut's Ella Grasso. When the Ninety-Sixth Congress convened in January 1979, Congresswoman Geraldine Ferraro was one of only 17 women among the 535 members of both houses and one of 10 Democratic female House members.

At forty-three, Ferraro skyrocketed into the national spotlight. *Time, U.S. News and World Report,* the *Washington Post,* and the *New York Times* became interested, featuring her as a "new" and thoroughly attractive face in the Congress. She made it clear that it was a Democratic face. Within the first few months, she became a good friend to Speaker Thomas P. O'Neill and a firm ally of Jimmy Carter. She also became a juggler, as all legislators must, balancing national responsibilities, constituency duties, and her own family obligations. Ferraro stressed that her goal would be community service and expressed the belief that her national role would help fulfill her constituents' needs, particularly the needs of the elderly and the disadvantaged. She gave as much time as possible to John and the children, deftly warding off journalistic queries on what her family thought of her absences most week nights by asking why that question was not put to male legislators with the same frequency.

The new member of Congress pragmatically balanced district interests with her conscience, although she frequently deferred to her perception of the electorate's interest during her first term, as is typical of new legislators. From a handful of Democratic women in the House, she soon found herself marked for better things. She frankly attributes much of her rapid rise in party circles to her sex, as she had her appointment as bureau chief. In 1983 she observed:

> Would I have gotten to where I am in the Congress in a little over four years if I weren't a woman? Again I'd like to think they recognized me as a genius but what happens is, the Speaker has twelve women and all these guys and invariably somebody will say "We need a Commission and don't forget the women," so they're reaching out to those twelve time and time again because that's all they've got. And they may not even reach out to the full twelve because the twelve may not all want to do it. Maybe five women might say "I want to move forward, I want to help the party, I want to get involved in this or that," so it becomes very obvious and you become very well known. Would this happen to a fellow? No, so there are advantages to being a woman in Congress, advantages and disadvantages.

She was given two committee assignments, to Public Works and Transportation and Post Office and Civil Service. Each carried her into two subcommittees, giving her a substantial number of opportunities to help district, county, and city. Among the specific items she worked on in her early career in Congress were the third water tunnel to provide New York City with adequate water sources into the next century, a zip code change to define her Ridgewood constituents as Queens and not Brooklyn residents, and the addition of questions on the census form in various foreign languages. The last measure showed a healthy respect for the 55 percent of her district who were of foreign stock.

Appointment to the Select Committee on Aging gave her another opportunity to serve her constituents. This was especially suitable because the residents of her district were some of the oldest in the nation. Social Security, fuel subsidies, tax breaks for the aging, and senior citizen housing became causes with which she became visibly and effectively identified. No cause was too small or too remote for her.

One of the most pleasant and rewarding tasks, she discovered, was bringing federal dollars to the district. She was especially proud of the grant of nearly $5 million from the Economic Development Administration for Astoria Studios. She proved very adept at this, and as one grant or loan fed on another, she was soon exercising a constituency clout rarely enjoyed in a freshman term.

Always a fine public speaker, she was often in demand throughout the district and the city. Within a few months of taking the oath she began to collect plaques, awards, scrolls, and testimonials by the wallful. Naturally gregarious, she enjoyed the accolades, and her enjoyment showed. She found it exciting to be on the dais with some of the nation's idols.

The two years allotted to House members spun by, and a new campaign was upon her. But 1980 was different from 1978—Ferraro's ally in her previous election, Jimmy Carter, was now the central player, vainly battling for his life against the superb media performance of Ronald Reagan. She enjoyed her role as a minor celebrity at the convention, introducing Morris Udall, the keynote speaker, in a speech that brought her briefly into tens of millions of homes. She also served as a key person marshalling delegate strength for the President.

In Ferraro's own campaign for reelection, her opponent was a peppery Conservative state legislator named Vito Batista, who had the endorsement of three New York political parties—the Republicans, the Conservatives, and the Right to Life party. Batista gave Geraldine Ferraro a tough fight. She won, defeating her opponent 58 to 41 percent. But it was a sad victory for her and for Democratic power in the nation. "It's going to make my job harder," she told a *Newsday* reporter right after the 1980 election. ". . . As a Democrat, I had access to the Democratic White House. With Reagan, I'm sure I won't have it."

In addition to losing the White House, the Democrats lost twelve Senate seats, thereby giving the Republicans a majority, and although the Democrats retained a majority in the House, they lost thirty-four seats in that body. Despite the fact that the number of women increased from sixteen to nineteen, nine were Republican, representing a net loss of one for the Democrats.

In January 1981 the Democrats needed Ferraro more than ever. She was a "good" Democrat; except for her primary challenge in 1978, she did not fight the party but rather served it loyally. After her primary victory, she offered the olive branch and remained staunchly true. She developed a close relationship with Speaker O'Neill, went to the meetings, took the assignments and—far from being the female to fill out the quota—was an effective and persuasive party pragmatist. That same year she was named chair of the Subcommittee on Human Resources and secretary of the House Democratic Caucus.

Ferraro advanced rapidly in party leadership ranks, enjoying the inner circle's confidence and trust. Her votes in the second term demonstrated that she was more her own person and more a *national* legislator than in the first. She earned respectable rankings—in the 80–89 percent range—from the Americans for Democratic Action falling below the 20 percent range in the eyes of the Americans for Conservative Action. Her hold on the district grew tighter. In 1982 she swept Republican opponent John J. Weigandt away 73 to 20 percent. She took no chances in this election, expending a reported $140,557 to Weigandt's $448.

In the new Congress, Ferraro won a seat on the influential Budget Committee, taking a leave of absence from her post on the House Post Office and Civil Service Committee. She continued her participation on the House Select Committee on the Aging and the Committee on Public Works, both of which were extremely important to her constituents.

As in her earlier terms of office, Ferraro focused on national and local concerns in her third term. She continued to pursue her interests in a wide variety of areas including assistance for the aging, women's and children's issues, equity in taxation, control of the federal budget deficit in general and defense spending in particular, federal aid to mass transit, reform of Social Security, issues of unemployment and job training.

In the spring of 1983, with congresswomen Barbara B. Kennelly (D-Conn) and Barbara A. Mikulski (D-Md), Ferraro undertook a fact-finding trip to the Middle East, including visits to Israel, Lebanon, and Cyprus. This was followed in early 1984 by a trip she undertook to investigate conditions in Costa Rica, El Salvador, Honduras, and Nicaragua. In each area, Ferraro endeavored to study the region's complex problems and their possible solutions. As might be expected, she was often critical of Reagan administration policies, including, for example, a delay in shipping warplanes to Israel and the U.S. abstention on a U.N. resolution calling for the withdrawal of all foreign forces from Cyprus and for peaceful negotiations. As a result of her trip to Central America, taken with Congresswoman Kennelly and Congressman Theodore Weiss (D-NY), Ferraro issued a call for support of the Contadora process for peaceful settlement of that region's problems and opposed isolating any nations in that area. She specifically condemned the U.S. mining of Nicaraguan harbors and all attempts by our nation to achieve victory in the area through the use of U.S. military forces.

During her entire tenure in Congress, Ferraro took a firm stand in support of peaceful solutions to the troubles in the "hot spots" of the globe, including repeated calls for peace in Northern Ireland. She also took a strong stand in support of the cause of Soviet Jewry, condemning Soviet repression of basic human rights and the right of Soviet Jews to emigrate to Israel.

Women's Issues

Congresswoman Geraldine Ferraro always has been a firm champion of equality for women in both the private and public sectors. She has been very critical of the Reagan administration's budgetary cutbacks and has noted that those in the area of social services had a particularly negative impact on assistance needed by women. At a 1981 Women in Crisis conference held in New York City, she urged those in attendance to turn their attentions on state and local government in order to take full advantage of programs available at that level.

Early in Reagan's first term Ferraro also attacked the president's plan to reduce federal government expenditures by eliminating many part-time positions in government service. She argued that as those were often relatively low-paying positions, the work would then be assumed by persons holding higher salaried positions, and the cutback would result in no real savings. In addition, however, she noted that this program was particularly onerous to women because they held such a significant percentage of these part-time positions.

As a member of the Select Committee on Aging, the congresswoman championed the cause of older women, noting that two-thirds of the elderly who are poverty-stricken are women. In addition, she told a conference sponsored by the New York chapter of the National Organization for Women, at which she was keynote speaker, that 60 percent of the unmarried women who are more than sixty-five years of age depend entirely on their Social Security checks for their income.[4]

She remains a firm supporter of the Equal Rights Amendment, which she believes assists women in three major ways: "job opportunity, equal pay, and fair retirement." She noted in 1982 that the "ERA would not solve all the problems which women, or men, face in our society, but it would create a climate of fairness to women in all aspects of our lives."[5]

As a legislator, Ferraro fought to retain the federal "flextime" system of employment, which was of special benefit to women who had to adjust their work schedules to their family responsibilities. In the fall of 1982, as chair of the Subcommittee on Human Resources and in conjunction with subcommittees chaired by congresswomen Patricia Schroeder and Mary Rose Oakar, Ferraro held hearings on "comparability"—that is, equal pay for equal work. She was highly critical of the Reagan administration's secretary of labor, who rejected an invitation to represent the administration's viewpoint on this issue.

During that same period, Ferraro chaired a House Democratic Caucus Task Force on Women's Economic Issues, which released a report on the economic plight of U.S. women. The report noted that, among other problems, women in the labor force only earn 60 percent of the salaries of their male counterparts, that among the elderly, two-and-one-half times as many women as men live in poverty, that three-quarters of those living below the poverty line are women and children, and that in 1981 the median earnings for families with female heads was less than $11,000 (less than half that of all families). In her introduction to that report, the congresswoman scored the Reagan administration for initiating cuts in programs that would improve "educational equity for women" while at the same time slashing the social programs upon which women and their families are dependent.[6]

In one of the most significant acts of her tenure in Congress, Ferraro, in February 1981, introduced the Private Pension Reform Act, which would amend the Employee Retirement Income Security Act in such a manner as to offer better service to women. Among its various provisions were lowering of the entrance age in pension plans to twenty-one years, protection for women who have to temporarily withdraw from the labor market to raise families, and improvements in survivor benefit rules. Her bill, which was part of the Economic Equity Act introduced at the same time, was reintroduced in 1983 and was passed unanimously by the House the following year, a vote the congresswoman termed "one of the most gratifying occasions in my career as a legislator."[7] In related areas, the congresswoman cosponsored legislation requiring the Veterans Administration to form a committee to ensure equal care for women veterans, and she supported the 1983 School Facilities Child Care Act, which was designed to offer after-school services for the so-called "latch-key" child.

Although the foregoing merely highlights the congresswoman's legislative service in the cause of women's and children's rights, it does illustrate her clear and consistent support of these issues, which has earned her the high esteem she enjoys among women's and other civil rights organizations.

The Quest for the Vice Presidency

As early as 1980, Congresswoman Geraldine A. Ferraro was under consideration as a potential running mate for Walter Mondale, John Glenn, or one of the other luminaries on the Democratic horizon. But 1983 was the year she left the orbit of attractive, competent Representative and entered the heady atmosphere of celebrity status.

Her face appeared on the cover of the *New York Times Magazine* in May

1983 in company with newly elected governor Mario Cuomo, Lee A. Iacocca, and a number of other Italian-American superstars. Gail Sheehy perceptively observed that a "magnetic field of warmth seems to arise out of her utter sincerity," a quality she shares with Antonetta. Everything a candidate should be seemed to be wrapped up in the trim package that was Geraldine Ferraro: exceptionally high intelligence, compassion, ambition, stamina, and the will to lead.

During the second half of 1983, she found herself besieged on every side by questioners who sought opinions on the candidates, the issues, and, above all, on her own candidacy for the second spot on the ticket. She shrugged these off good-humoredly, little believing that the lightning bolt would land anywhere near her. Ferraro got an inkling of how serious her potential candidacy might be in November 1983 when a group of influential liberal Democratic women invited her to dinner to discuss the possibilities with her. After several hours of conversation, she was flattered but remained unconvinced that a female candidacy was viable in 1984. She later wrote that "the idea still seemed off the wall to me."[8] During spring 1984, the race for the Democratic presidential nomination resolved itself into a struggle among Walter "Fritz" Mondale, vice president during the Carter administration and twice Carter's running mate, Colorado's Senator Gary Hart, an old George McGovern ally, and Reverend Jesse Jackson, the first black presidential candidate.

By the end of June, Mondale had begun to interview potential running mates, including one black, one Hispanic, and two women. Ferraro was one of these last and in the end chosen. Mondale announced her selection on July 12, 1984. In declaring his choice, the former vice president said that "Gerry has excelled in everything she's tried, from law school at night to being a tough prosecutor to winning a difficult election, to winning positions of leadership and respect in the Congress."[9]

Mondale's choice was historic and pragmatic. Never before had a woman been selected to run for this office. Indeed, few women—except Shirley Chisholm and several small party candidates—ever had seriously considered or been seriously considered for either of the highest offices. Mondale's choice also sought to capitalize on the "gender gap," which showed U.S. women drifting away from men in political activity, particularly with respect to sympathy for President Reagan. Mondale's decision also was calculated to appeal to the ethnic electorate, especially Italian Americans, who generally supported Republicans on national issues and leaders, and was expected to block the leakage of Catholic voters to the Reagan-Bush camp.[9A]

Ferraro was immediately subjected to extremely close scrutiny of her campaign expenditures for the 1978 congressional election as well as her financial relationship with her husband's real estate business. She spent an inordinate amount of time defending herself and her husband against a host of charges. The net effect of the entire financial affair was to divert her energies during July and August away from campaigning and to dull some of the luster of her candidacy.[10]

No sooner had the campaign gotten fully under way on the Labor Day weekend than she was the target of a massive attack by members of the hierarchy of the Roman Catholic church. Religion already had been injected into the campaign by all sides. Jackson was a minister, Mondale described himself as "a minister's kid," Reagan made frequent references to the relationship between religion and politics, and Reverend Jerry Falwell's Moral Majority was unabashedly dedicated to pulpit politics. The form religion took in Ferraro's case was the abortion issue. During House debate on Federal funding for abortions for the poor in June 1979, Congresswoman Ferraro had spoken to this issue on the floor of the House, expressing the position that would accurately reflect her 1984 views.

> As a Catholic, I accept the premise that fertilized ovum is a baby. I have been blessed with the gift of faith; but others have not. I have no right to impose my beliefs on them. I firmly believe, given my current situation, that I could never have an abortion. I am not so sure, however, if I were the victim of rape and faced with a pregnancy question whether or not I would be so self-righteous. The cost of putting an unwanted child through the system far outweighs the cost of funding these procedures. It is easy to placate a special interest group which is flexing its political muscle. It is the easy vote, I repeat, but not the courageous one.[11]

Moreover, on September 30, 1982, she and two other Catholic representatives had circulated a letter among the legislators of their faith. This called for a meeting to "show us that the Catholic position is not monolithic and that there can be a range of personal and political responses to the issue."[12]

Both of these statements reached deeply into the beliefs and authority of the Roman Catholic hierarchy. In early September, Boston's Archbishop Bernard Law, speaking for seventeen other New England Catholic prelates, called abortion "the critical issue in this campaign." He said that the statement was aimed at all candidates, but added, "I think Geraldine Ferraro is a candidate."[13] New York's Archbishop John J. O'Connor took issue with Ferraro's 1982 letter by quoting the pope: "Abortion is death. It is the killing of an innocent creature."[14] He unequivocally contradicted the letter's contention that the Catholic position is not monolithic. "There is no variance, there is no flexibility, there is no leeway as far as the Catholic church says."[15] Interestingly, George Bush and Fritz Mondale shared Ferraro's abortion views in general yet did not suffer such public attention. Perhaps because Ferraro in fact could have an abortion, her potential as a role model invited greater public scrutiny.

Her responses to her clerical critics were respectful and clear-cut, but they hurt her politically or at least were of no significant assistance to the campaign. This controversy and the financial one drained away her energy and support. Yet during the campaign, it was clear that she could bat against any pitcher, and some of her most effective campaigning was against the president. In Ohio in September she used her teaching background to score on Reagan in a Toledo school, grading the president with A for a neat desk, B + for making friends, but C for effort and D for caring. She recommended he not be promoted. It was a clever artifice and helped underscore her underdog, hometown image.[16] In Philadelphia a few days later, she said, "I go slightly berserk when I see that people think that Reagan is a leader and that he's a man's man. When it comes to arms control it takes a leader not only to stand up to the Russians. It takes a leader to sit down with them and negotiate an agreement."[17]

Against her vice presidential opponent, George Bush, she was equally tough and vigorous, trading charges and jibes. Her mettle was fully tested in the first vice presidential debate involving a female candidate. The vice president, a former director of the Central Intelligence Agency and a U.N. ambassador with other foreign policy experience, was a formidable foe. The ninety-minute debate in Philadelphia on October 11 was a serious exchange of policy differences for the most part, but the candidates were required to answer pointed questions about their finances and tax difficulties as well. Geraldine Ferraro did bristle on one occasion regarding Bush's "patronizing attitude," as she called it, about her knowledge of foreign policy.[18] This was her Achilles heel because her congressional work had been in the domestic arena with little development of foreign policy save in the context of Middle Eastern, Latin American, and Cypriot concerns. She had admitted this to writer Gail Sheehy in an exchange Ferraro later related in her book. "Tell me a weakness," Sheehy had asked. "'Foreign policy,' I promptly offered." She called this "one of my dumber moves."[19]

The significance of Geraldine Ferraro's role in the 1984 election is in its broader implications. At best, she minimally influenced the eventual outcome of the race (most vice presidential nominees have relatively little impact on election outcomes), but her participation as a candidate had an immeasurable impact on the future of U.S. politics. Some have suggested that choosing Geraldine A. Ferraro as his running mate may have been Walter Mondale's "most significant contribution to American politics."[20] Ferraro proved, if she proved anything at all, that a woman could stand up to the country.

Richard Moe, a one-time Mondale associate and a perceptive political observer, summed up the election by indicating that the nation had reelected a president who had brought them peace and prosperity and who, in addition, had run an outstanding campaign with virtually no serious blunders.[21] When the Democrats surveyed the election, they had little to encourage them beyond small gains in the Senate and small losses in the House. They enjoyed voting majorities among the Jewish electorate, among those with less than a high school education, among those of no religion, and among Hispanics, blacks, and union households.[22] Otherwise, every age group, white men and women, Protestants and Catholics, and forty-nine states gave Reagan an overwhelming landslide. Even the Ninth C.D. in Queens and Italian-American women gave their votes to the incumbents,[23] which may fortify the argument that voters cast ballots for Reagan or Mondale and not for Bush or Ferraro.

Twin setbacks hit the Ferraro-Zaccaro family after the defeat. The House Ethics Committee in December voted 10–2 to approve a document that stated Ferraro had violated the Ethics in Government Act by failing to disclose her husband's finances because her assets and his were so closely bound.[24] However, the report was softened by the committee's assertion that the failure was not intentional, which the congresswoman interpreted as a vindication.[25] The following month, John Zaccaro pleaded guilty to a misdemeanor charge involving his real estate dealings. He blamed the investigation of his activities on the "microscopic" examination of his business that commenced with his wife's nomination.

Geraldine Ferraro was disappointed. She felt the Italian-American community had let her down, thought her church had used a double standard in dealing with her, and resented certain media attacks that she saw as either untrue or irrelevant.[26]

Conclusion

It is difficult to predict the political future of Geraldine Ferraro. Some had speculated that she might try to unseat New York Senator Alfonse D'Amato in 1986, but she did not choose to run. Whatever career path she may ultimately choose, it cannot be denied that she has already made a most significant contribution to U.S. politics. As a congresswoman, she receives an A for both effort and caring.

Perhaps her rise to national prominence was too fast, or perhaps the nation's expectations were unrealistic. Whatever the case, Geraldine Ferraro has made an indelible impact on the U.S. political scene by chipping away at religious and ethnic barriers and by taking a huge chunk out of the barrier that traditionally has prevented women from reaching high political office in this nation. There is already discussion in the media and among party leaders concerning the possibility of running a woman for Vice President in 1988, perhaps this time on the Republican party ticket. It is far too soon to hazard a guess concerning the likelihood of such an occurrence, and indeed, it remains to be seen how *permanent* the impact of the Ferraro nomination will be, in the sense of it being the first of many such nominations. Nevertheless, with the many increases in nomination and election of women to high public office, there is every reason to remain optimistic concerning the nomination of future women vice presidential, and indeed, presidential candidates.

Notes

1. All direct quotations throughout this chapter, except where otherwise noted, together with much background material, are based on a series of interviews conducted by the authors with Geraldine Ferraro, Antonetta Ferraro, Carl Ferraro, and John Zaccaro. The material upon which the campaign of 1978 is based consists of interviews with Patricia M. Reilly, Ferraro's aide, and Richard McLaughlin, aide to Alfred Dellibovi.

2. *The New York Times,* July 26, 1984, A20.

3. Richard McLaughlin, interview with Arthur J. Hughes.

4. *The New York Times,* November 2, 1981.

5. Congresswoman Ferraro Press Release, August 26, 1982.

6. "Expanding the Role of Women in Our Economy," Report of the Task Force on Women's Economic Issues, 1982.

7. Press Conference Statement, May 22, 1984.

8. Geraldine A. Ferraro with Linda Bird Francke, *Ferraro: My Story* (New York: Bantam Books, 1985), 73.

9. *The New York Times,* July 13, 1984, A1.

9A. For an interesting analysis of many of these points, see Paul C. Light and Celinda Lake, The Election: Candidates, Strategies, and Decisions," in Michael Nelson, ed., *The Elections of 1984* (Washington, D.C.: C. Q. Press, 1985), 105, 106.

10. *The New York Times,* August 22, 1984, A1, B5, B6,B7; *Daily News* (New York), August 22, 1984, 1, 3, 20, 28; *The New York Times,* August 16, 1984, A1, B11.

11. House of Representatives debate on Federal funding for abortions for the poor, June 1979, quoted in *New York Times,* July 13, 1984, A10.

12. Quoted in *New York Times,* September 11, 1984, A26.

13. *The New York Times,* September 6, 1984, B13.

14. *The New York Times,* September 10, 1984, B9.

15. Ibid. Also see the excerpts from a speech made by the then archbishop John J. O'Connor quoted in *New York Times,* October 16, 1984, B2.

16. *The New York Times,* September 12, 1984, B9.

17. *The New York Times,* September 19, 1984, B9.

18. *Daily News* (New York), October 12, 1984, 3.

19. Ferraro, *Ferraro,* 77.

20. Light and Lake, 106–107.

21. *The New York Times,* November 16, 1984, A24.

22. Light, "The Election," 106.

23. Ferraro, *Ferraro,* 313; *Newsweek Election Special,* November-December 984, 6.

24. *The New York Times,* December 5, 1984, A1.

25. Ibid., A20.

26. "A Credible Candidacy and Then Some," in *Time Election Special,* November 19, 1984, 84–85.

Margaret M. Heckler: Student Legislator to Ambassador

ARTHUR A. BELONZI

Ambassador Margaret M. Heckler, champion of women's rights, former congresswoman and secretary of health and human services, was born Margaret Mary O'Shaughnessy. The dynamic and determined feisty former legislator was born in Flushing, an unassuming area in Queens, New York City, on June 21, 1931, to Irish Catholic immigrants, Bridget McKean and John O'Shaughnessy.[1] Heckler's mother was devoutly religious, with a practical nature. Her father was a well-liked, conscientious, friendly doorman at a New York City hotel.

In the 1930s and 1940s Heckler attended St. Bridget's Grammar School and Dominican High School, where she was an outstanding student. She also was involved in a number of other activities; piano-playing in particular was on her list, and she participated in a variety of church activities.

Part of her uniqueness might be attributed to being an only child: without siblings, particularly male, it appears that her parents focused on Margaret their own "immigrant's dream" of success in America. The drive to follow the dream led Margaret away from the traditional role of a female child in an immigrant's house. She frequently discussed controversial political issues with family and friends, something most young women of her background did not do.

Growing up during the time of the Depression and World War II, young Heckler never lost her parents' conviction that hard work was good for the soul and would eventually lead to success. This was the immigrants' credo, the American dream, and a pattern in her political and personal life. Heckler inherited the unconquerable winning spirit so frequently demonstrated by Irish Americans in political history.

Margaret was well liked and personable as a teenager. When entering educational, cultural, or personal commitments, she was reasonable, intelligent, and enthusiastic, but cautious as well. Growing up in the 1930s and 1940s, Margaret had to adhere to a rigid social code. Even if in her parents' eyes she was fulfilling a son's role, in society she still had to appear feminine. This necessity did not inhibit Margaret's assertiveness or leadership qualities; it did assist her in planning her future carefully and pragmatically.

The confident high school senior was awarded a full scholarship to Albertus Magnus College, a small Catholic college in New Haven, Connecticut. Though separation from her parents was difficult, the independent and determined future ambassador to Ireland decided to make a "go of it," and she soon settled into college life. Heckler commenced her collegiate studies in 1950 and majored in political science.[2] She attacked the curriculum with customary gusto, performing well in her studies.

However, this gregarious woman did not neglect the extracurricular aspects of college life. In 1951 she was elected to the annual three-day Assembly of the Connecticut Intercollegiate Student Legislature, and greatly enjoyed the experience. In 1952 she "threw her hat in the ring" and campaigned for the speakership of the Student Legislature,[3] a position not previously held by a woman.

Breaking new political ground excited the future congresswoman. She and another college student, John M. Heckler, carefully analyzed her chances of victory. He acted as her campaign manager, and together they designed her political strategy. It was relatively simplistic in design. They decided to emphasize her outgoing and friendly personality; Margaret was well versed in the major issues facing the legislative body, and used her debating skills frequently, understanding that challengers should be the aggressors. John and Margaret thoroughly advertised her name on posters, flyers, and handouts—she understood the significance of publicity early in her career. Six months of exhausting work resulted in success—the election was a runaway. They enjoyed the fruits of victory as she won the Student Legislature position with an overwhelming majority.[4]

Speaker O'Shaughnessy memorized Robert's *Rules of Order.* She clearly grasped the significance of controlling a raucous group of delegates by conquering and rigorously enforcing parliamentarian procedures.[5] She kept order, and this impressed the students. Though Margaret had half-seriously considered becoming a concert pianist, the attraction to politics now became compelling. Victory was satisfying, and Margaret correctly reasoned that the role of women in politics would be greatly expanding. More women were voting and this could alter elections. Margaret felt that in the future much work would be done in the legislatures on women's rights in the labor force, in credit, and before the law.

Characteristically positive and practical, she concluded that it was through the mastery of law that she would enter government service. In addition, government and politics satisfied other personal needs: the altruistic aspect of her nature would be pleased. Women and other members of the population struggling for a "place in the sun" would benefit by her concern. By studying law she would learn the mechanical procedures utilized in government and bring an expertise in understanding what constitutionally could or could not be achieved. Politically, the study of law was a definite plus. In combining the noble with the utilitarian, the former political science major proved there was a place for women in the "house" of legislature.

Heckler enthusiastically spent the 1952-1953 academic year as an exchange student at the University of Leyden in the Netherlands. Upon her return to Albertus Magnus College in the summer of 1953, she received a Bachelor of Arts degree. On August 29, she and John M. Heckler, her campaign strategist, were married.

In September 1954 she enrolled at Boston College Law School. Starting another stage of her adult life, Margaret systematically and skillfully delved into her studies. Her pioneer instincts were appeased for the moment: Heckler was the only woman in her class, but she eagerly took the job of editing the law review and handily won the moot court competition three times!

In 1956 Heckler graduated sixth in her class. Awarded an LL.B. degree with honors, she was admitted to practice law in Massachusetts and before the U.S. Supreme Court. By now the Hecklers lived in Wellesley, Massachusetts, and had started raising a family, but Margaret was also an attorney and anxious to practice her profession. In the mid-1950s there were few positions for women in the legal profession, especially in the Boston area. Therefore this resourceful young attorney opened a law firm with her friends.[6] This law firm was designed to bring efficient and effective assistance to clients, and to keep clients well informed. According to Margaret's management principles, the attorneys must be available at all times to the clients.

Simultaneously, she began working as a volunteer in the local Republican Club. She assisted ineffective Republican candidates in personal and organizational problems, mapping out fundraising techniques, and advising them to pursue weaknesses in their opponents' strategy and to "tighten up" on staff loyalty. Her energy and common sense proved valuable, as she was a lawyer by training (that is, a member of a profession with access to political life), her public career was initiated.

Heckler was secure in the conviction that she would be a political success. She was confident by nature, ambitious, and enjoyed the support of her friends. Women were becoming more prominent in American politics, doors were opening, financially she was secure, and she had access to a superior organizing machine which included her husband John.

She quickly became a representative on the Wellesley Republican Town Committee and remained a member of the committee from 1958 through 1966. She also sat on the board of the historic Massachusetts Governor's Council. In 1962, when she ran for the council, the Republican bosses and party workers criticized her efforts for political recognition. The majority of them considered her a maverick, because of her independent approach to issues; Margaret felt that as a woman, she brought with her a new and exacting dimension, one that would attract voters. Again, with the help of her husband as chief strategist, she ran a moderate to liberal campaign. She was interested in women receiving equal rights in job opportunities, in personal and commercial credit, and in gaining access to political party management and election positions. As a politician she was informed, knowledgeable, interested in the public welfare, loyal to the party, and a proven winner. She was in fact a leader. With the slogan, "You need a Heckler on the Governor's Council," Margaret's bid for triumph paid off.[7]

Juggling family and career was not simple and at times conflicts arose and priorities changed. To a degree family life had to suffer, but Margaret was a dynamo of energy and she usually kept the candle "burning at both ends," sometimes putting in fifteen- to sixteen-hour days. The Heckler household was carefully organized and timetables had to be kept. Order had to be a primary ingredient in everyday affairs.

Heckler was proud that hard work, careful planning, legal knowledge, and freedom from quid pro quo deals placed her on the eight-member Governor's Council. The council was an advisory body, which advised the governor on contracts and bids dealing with public projects. Heckler's vote often broke ties.

In 1964 she was reelected easily. During this stint on the council, scandals discredited the work of the board, but Heckler was unscathed by the charges of corruption.

Local politics served Heckler well, but social concern and ambition would soon lead her to national politics and Congress. Radical activities and disruptions in U.S. society—assassinations, escalation of the commitment in Vietnam, the changing role of women, and the restlessness of college students—all concerned Margaret.[8] She made up her mind to run for Congress in her home district, Massachusett's Tenth District. Politically, Wellesley was Republican—moderate to liberal on social issues and moderate on economic ones. In terms of real income, the town residents are upper middle class. Heckler's home was a staunch supporter of the perennial favorite, former Republican speaker of the House Joseph W. Martin. Determined to increase the number of women in national politics, she defied the governor of Massachusetts, John Volpe. Over his objections but acknowledging her inexperience, she entered the Republican primary against Martin.

She proved equal to the exhausting task ahead and was a tireless, assertive campaigner. Knowing well that to directly and harshly criticize the popular Martin would not be wise, she shrewdly avoided personal attacks.[9] Instead, she pointed out that the Tenth District deserved a full-time representative. Only with this type of devotion would the people of the district receive justice. Only with this commitment would their interests be protected and expanded.

During the preceding session of Congress, Martin had been absent for approximately 50 percent of the meetings. Equipped with this information, reciting the need for accessibility in government, she emphasized her youth, energy, and desire to serve. Heckler won the Republican primary in September 1966 by 3,200 votes. In November of the same year she beat the Democratic opponent—labor lawyer Patrick H. Harrington, Jr.—with 51.1 percent of the vote.[10] A close vote, but victory nonetheless. This would be her closest race until she lost the seat in 1982. However, the significance of the victory lay elsewhere. Congresswoman Heckler was the first woman to be elected to Congress from Massachusetts due to her own efforts and merits.[11] Additionally, in 1966 women were "on the move" politically in the United States, and Heckler not only reflected the liberation movement but consciously sought to be a trailblazer.[12] She intentionally worked to get women to register and vote for her candidacy. In December she acknowledged the fact that women placed her in Congress. Congresswoman Heckler became a spokeswoman for the Equal Rights Amendment and other women's issues. By 1966 Heckler was a smooth blend of principled congresswoman and practical politician.

On January 3, 1967, she installed a toll-free telephone between her office on Capitol Hill and her district in Massachusetts. She made herself accessible and accountable to the voters of the Tenth District. For both family and political reasons, the newly elected congresswoman returned from Washington, D.C. to Wellesley every week. The indefatigable Heckler continued this practice throughout her congressional years.

It was perhaps appropriate that her initial speech on the floor of the House concerned the civil rights of a Czech-born naturalized citizen who resided in the Tenth District. Her first committee assignment was a seat on the Government Operations and Veterans' Affairs Committee.[13] She served this committee with enthusiasm for sixteen years, eventually becoming the second-ranking Republican on the Veterans Committee. She also was appointed to the subcommittees on Education, Training, and Employment as well as on Hospitals and Health Care. These assignments would prove extremely valuable for her future. As success rolled on, she would hold seats on Banking and Commerce, Science and Technology, Agriculture, and Joint Economic Committees.

During her sixteen years in the House of Representatives, she became the ninth-ranking Republican of the Science and Technology Committee and was vice chair on the Investments, Jobs, and Prices Subcommittee. Articulate, legalistic, and combative, Heckler worked effectively to get numerous bills passed that were concerned with veterans' benefits, centers for the aging, federally backed child-care centers, education- and welfare-oriented programs. She remained an excellent political manipulator and skilled debator. Many pieces of congressional legislation do not have her name on them because she saw her job in terms of persuading, arguing, and discussing bills rather than authoring measures. She was a leading spokeswoman and adviser rather than a leading writer of legislation. She appeared to enjoy the vocal aspects of political representation, not the tedious and exacting work of writing a bill. Heckler could best lead, direct, and inform the Republican party and her constituency by exploiting her strongest talents.

As her knowledge of the rules and procedures of the House became part of everyday practice, her catalytic qualities grew in sophistication, and she became an effective legislator, particularly in women's rights issues. However, veterans' affairs and child welfare measures were becoming increasingly important to the representative from New England.

During her tenure in the House, Heckler was a leader in the move for funding centers on aging in Veterans' Administration hospitals throughout the United States. She sponsored bills to support counseling for Vietnam veterans who demonstrated personal and social adjustment problems. Congresswoman Heckler believed that government-financed programs would accelerate the veterans' assimilation into mainstream U.S. life.[14] At times her views clashed with the Republican president. Although Heckler remained friendly with the Nixon administration, she antagonized this relationship when she publicly attacked and condemned President Nixon's veto of the federally sponsored day-care facilities for children of working mothers. She was of the opinion that such a veto would mean that justice would not be achieved for either children or women, that women's rights in the marketplace as well as their social rights would be jeopardized if Congress failed to override the president's veto.

Heckler, not admitting defeat, battled for the need of a day care plank in the platform at the 1972 Republican National Convention. In 1973 she co-sponsored a bill pushing for a national day care nursery system. She felt at home fighting for these issues; she knew when, where, and how to apply pressure, and she succeeded eventually. Both of these bills became law, due in no small measure to her persuading other House members to vote for the bills.

Meanwhile she was firmly entrenched in the House as a seasoned and experienced warrior. She was not to be taken for granted or taken lightly, even by the leaders of the Republican party. She fully realized the "way to get along is to go along" with her party, and a proportional mixture of party loyalty, commitment to her liberal constituency (a district that now contained more blue-collar Democratic areas[15]), and personal political opportunism added up to reelections and political success.

In 1978 Representative Heckler co-sponsored a congressional resolution extending the deadline for the ratification of the Equal Rights Amendment. This amendment, which once and forever would implement the concepts of "inalienable rights" of women, "equality of opportunity," "equality before the law" was in danger of failing the ratification procedure. In 1980 she tried to cajole the conservative wing of the Republican Party to endorse the legislation. She did not succeed in these endeavors, but not for lack of effort. Undaunted, she renewed her commitments for women's rights and aided in setting up a National Center for the Prevention and Control of Rape, in establishing centers for battered wives and children, and in sponsoring plans to protect pension rights of working women on maternity leave. This is one of the areas where the resident of Wellesley remained consistently liberal.

In 1974 she drafted the Equal Credit Opportunity Act. This established equality of credit approvals for women who sought loans for mortgages and personal reasons. In 1977 she joined the Democratic Representative from Brooklyn, New York, Elizabeth Holtzman, in forming and functioning as co-chairs of the Congressional Caucus for Women's Issues. She served through the 1982 session. The objective of the caucus was to convince more women to enter government service and to promote women's rights legislation. However, the congresswoman's stand against abortion prevented some groups from nationally endorsing Heckler. Representative Heckler believed that abortion was immoral and not a satisfactory alternative to unwanted pregnancies; that the rights of the unborn are to be respected as much as women's rights.

Nonetheless, her sincerity on this issue was recognized by the Democratic Speaker of the House, Representative Carl Albert of Oklahoma. He appointed her to the National Commission on the Observance of the International Women's Year in 1975 and also appointed her as the first congresswoman to visit the People's Republic of China.

With fingers on the pulse of her constituents' opinions, she approved urban redevelopment projects, subsidies, and grants for public transportation, advocated support for consumer protection measures, tax reform, and environmental preservation standards, and sponsored measures to safeguard the health and welfare of senior citizens.

In terms of national defense, she originally supported Nixon (in 1980 this issue almost lost her the election). She soon became quite negative about the wisdom of Nixon's Vietnamization program and publicly requested the president to withdraw U.S. troops from that country. Was her position based on principle or political expedience? Or was Heckler following her concept of democracy? She firmly believed that a Representative should reflect her or his constituents' wishes. Nonetheless, her motives were not entirely clear. On other defense issues such as legislating more funds for the military, development of the B70 bomber, nuclear-powered aircraft carriers, and the MX missile program, the congresswoman voted a decisive no!

Perhaps the most interesting aspect of Ambassador Heckler's political career is that she crossed party lines in her voting record. She frequently voted on either side of the aisle in supporting legislative oversight and investigative measures. She remained moderate to liberal in her orientation. Throughout her years in the House, the Americans for Democratic Action, a liberal political group, rated her performance from 48 to 74 percent. On the other side of the political spectrum, the Americans for Conservative Action rated her performance between 12 and 48 percent. Congresswoman Heckler never received the highest liberal rating, but she did receive among the lowest ratings on the conservative side. During the Ninety-fourth Congress she voted with her Republican colleagues 34 percent of the time and with the bipartisan faction 82 percent of the time. This voting record is consistent with the political liberal leanings of Massachusetts and the Tenth District in particular.

As she held the congressional seat unopposed, or won by a substantial margin, she was raising three children—Belinda, a writer; Alison, a musician and composer; and John, a Washington stockbroker who is pursuing a business similar to his father's. (The Hecklers were divorced in the spring of 1985.)

When one views her House victories and her single loss in 1982, interesting patterns emerge. The eight-term congresswoman spent much more on campaigns than did her opponents. In 1980, for example, in her campaign against Democrat Robert E. McCarthy, she spent $264,688 to $158,110 for the opposition. In 1978 against John J. Marino her expenses ran to $210,730 compared to $78,848 for the losing candidate. She obviously was an astute fund-raiser and knew the value of money in campaigning.[16]

In terms of popular voting appeal, the congresswoman received from 60.6 to 100 percent of the votes cast between the years 1968 and 1980. (The only exception was in 1970, when the Republican Heckler received 57 percent of the votes, a solid majority, but her weakest return during these years.) See Table 5.1 for a list of Heckler's Tenth District opponents, the votes cast, and percentages received by the candidates.

Another pattern emerges—Heckler usually ran against liberal Democrats who were either Irish-American Catholics or Italo-American Catholics. She never had a woman as a political opponent.

The only loss she experienced was in 1982 when Democrat Barney Frank beat the pro-ERA congresswoman by 121,802 votes to 82,804. She received 40.5 percent of the total votes cast. The practical reason for her defeat was the gerrymandering of the Tenth District. By 1982 Massachusetts was required to lose one congressional district and because Democrats composed the clear majority of the state legislature, it became obvious the loss would

Table 5.1
Massachusetts' Tenth Congressional District, 1968–1982

Year	Candidates	Votes Received	Total	Percent of Total
1968	Margaret Heckler	138,220	205,173	67.4
	Edmund Denis	66,949		32.6
1970	Margaret Heckler	102,895	180,398	57.0
	Bertram A. Yaffe	77,497		43.0
1972	Margaret Heckler	161,708	161,708	100.0
	Uncontested	–		–
1974	Margaret Heckler	99,993	155,868	64.2
	Barry F. Monahan	55,871		35.8
1976	Margaret Heckler	176,604	176,604	100.0
	Uncontested	–		–
1978	Margaret Heckler	102,080	166,957	61.1
	John J. Marino	64,868		38.9
1980	Margaret Heckler	85,629	131,794	60.6
	Robert E. McCarthy	46,165		39.4
1982	Margaret Heckler	82,804	204,615	40.5
	Barney Frank	121,802		59.5

Source: See note 17.

be inflicted upon the Republicans. It was decided the northern part of the Tenth District would be added to the overwhelming Democratic 4th. Therefore, Wellesley, Natick, and Foxboro were absorbed into the east end of the Fourth District—the Brookline, Newton, and Waltham section. In addition to this structural maneuver, the well-known and consistently liberal challenger, Frank, was frequently rated as high as 97 on the ADA scale. Barney Frank was the easy victor. Whether Heckler would have been defeated without this "redistricting" effort is debatable. The seasoned professional, who for sixteen years represented a district with a population in 1981 of 523,101 and who brought more than $4 million in urban renewal grants to her district, might have defeated her Democratic opponent.[18] These accomplishments, when coupled with her fairly liberal voting record, might have won the congresswoman a seventh term. However, Congressman Frank contended that Margaret Heckler followed the Reagan line in 1981, and this was overt support for his economic policies, particularly his defense spending. Heckler changed her position regarding several Reagan economic proposals, trying to balance the changing views of her constituency, Republican party demands, and her own personal beliefs on major issues.

Heckler protested the redistricting. She appealed to the voters to look at the record and witness for themselves that through five presidents she voted independently but in a manner consistent with the wishes of the people in the Tenth District. This, after all, the Republican campaigner contended, is what "representative government" is all about. Furthermore, she generally supported and defended measures dealing with human values over institutional values. For example, on October 5, 1981, in the House, she emphatically demanded "that creating a new program for sugar growers was unthinkable while the elderly, the poor, and students were forced by budget cuts to lose federal benefits."[19] In 1980 she opposed moves to cut revenue sharing, which would have a negative effect on state programs dealing with the administration of human services.[20] The congressional election seemed to be more a Democratic and liberal victory rather than a Heckler defeat.

Through the late 1960s, the 1970s and the early 1980s, Heckler accumulated several significant personal awards. In 1965 she received the Outstanding Young Woman of America award. In 1984 she was selected as the Mother of the Year, and in 1985 she won the National Women's Economic Alliance Excellence in Leadership award. Her professional credentials added further to her stature. Margaret M. Heckler is a member of the Women's Republican Club of Massachusetts, the Boston American Bar Association, and the Massachusetts Trial Lawyers Association. Among her Academic awards are honorary doctorates in the humanities from Northeastern University and Emmanuel College and in law from Stonehill College, Regis College, Albertus Magnus College, Boston College, and Southeastern Massachusetts University.

While accumulating these awards and piling victory upon victory in Congress, she suddenly experienced defeat. Nonetheless, the loss in the congressional election of 1982 was certainly not her political obituary. After Secretary John Schweicker stepped down from the position, President Reagan nominated her for the position of secretary for health and human services. She accepted the nomination. Her testimony before the Senate Committee on Labor and Human Services was interesting.[21] On March 3, 1983, with her children and cousins from Limerick and Cork counties in Ireland present, she stated that her double goal as secretary of health and human services would be to "protect human life and preserve the civil rights of handicapped persons." Senator Lowell Weicker of Connecticut said her support would be administrative and not legislative in style. In fact, the senior senator was of the opinion that while a congresswoman she had voted against expanding funds into several programs sponsored by the committee and the Department of Health and Human Services. Heckler replied that "legislation and funding" may or may not be the solution to certain problems. She was approved by the committee for the position.[22]

Secretary Heckler served capably for two-and-one-half years. She was secretary of a department with the third-highest budget in contemporary political life—the budget for 1984 was $274 billion. Only the budgets of the United States and the Soviet Union are greater. This bureaucracy employs more than 142,000 people and serves 50 million people throughout the nation.

Heckler walked a tightrope as secretary of health and human services between administration policy and the needs of the people her department was intended to serve. The Reagan administration was frequently accused of indifference and even hostility toward this department; Heckler, although not strenuously criticizing the administration's views, tried to persuade the elderly, doctors, hospitals, and antipoverty groups that she represented their interests despite the administration's attitude. As secretary, Heckler supported, among other items:

1. Tax credit for day care
2. Stronger laws to compel payment of child support obligations
3. Additional research on Alzheimer's Disease
4. Money to combat Acquired Immunity Deficiency Syndrome (requests cut back by OMB)
5. Use of aerospace technology to help disabled people (this plan was presented in the spring of 1985 at the Paris Air Show)

Her White House critics argued that she failed to rally public support for the administration's proposed cuts in the department's budget, and she certainly did not follow the party line exclusively. On the other hand, the secretary's liberal critics cried that she was not active enough in legislative matters: few pieces of legislation concerning the needs of the disabled, elderly, and the like carried her assent; she was preoccupied with administrative busy work or general, sweeping endorsements, which failed to solve particular problems.

After two-and-one-half years as secretary of health and human services, her liberal views having conflicted with administrative aides, Heckler left the position because of White House pressure. On October 2, 1985, President Reagan appointed her U.S. ambassador to Ireland.[23] At first, the White House staff resisted her appointment, and the former secretary herself considered the appointment a demotion, but soon her pragmatic nature manifested itself and she hailed the Republican president as a "great communicator."[24] She viewed the appointment as important to women and to Irish Americans. In her new position she intended to be a "shrewd and combative envoy."[25]

Upon her appointment, William V. Shannon, author of *Irish Americans* and other books and articles on Irish Americans and himself a former U.S. ambassador to Ireland (1977–1981), said he thought Heckler's appointment would be received extremely well in Ireland, and she is indeed serving ably in this capacity.

Notes

1. Charles Moritz, et al., *Current Biography 1983* (New York: H. W. Wilson, 1983), 182.

2. Ibid.

3. Ibid.

4. Ibid., 185.

5. *Wall Street Journal,* January 13, 1985, 2.

6. Moritz, *Current Biography,* 183.

7. M. Barone, et al., *Almanac of American Politics* (Washington, D.C.: National Journal, 1982), 510.

8. For an excellent treatment of congresswomen in general and Heckler in particular during the 1970s, see Essie E. Lee, *Women in Congress* (New York: Julian Messner, 1979).

9. See *Parade Magazine,* January 15, 1967, 28.

10. R. M. Scammon, et al., *America Votes 14: A Handbook of Contemporary American Election Statistics, Election Research Center* (Washington, D.C.: Congressional Quarterly, 1983), 201.

11. See Peggy Lamson, *Few Are Chosen: American Women in Political Life Today* (Boston: Houghton Mifflin, 1968).

12. Ibid.

13. The numerous references to committee meetings published in the *Congressional Quarterly* 1970–1981 are outstanding for an analysis of the opinions held by Heckler.

14. Jack Lyness' article, "Margaret Heckler, Republican Representative from Massachusetts," in Ralph Nader, ed., *Citizens Look at Congress* (Washington, D.C.: Grossman Publishing, 1972), 22, offers interesting comments on these issues.

15. See the socioeconomic breakdown of the Tenth District in Barone, *Almanac of American Politics,* 511.

16. Ibid.

17. Scammon, R. M., et al., *American Voter 15: A Handbook of Contemporary American Statistics, Election Research Center* (Washington, D.C.: Congressional Quarterly, 1983), 175.

18. *Congressional Quarterly Almanac 1983* (Washington, D.C.: Congressional Quarterly, 1983), 390.

19. *Congressional Quarterly Almanac 1980* (Washington, D.C.: Congressional Quarterly, 1980), 154.

20. Ibid.

21. U.S. Congress, Senate, *Hearing before the Committee on Labor and Human Resources,* 98th Cong., 1st sess., March 3, 1983.

22. Ibid.

23. Robert Pear, "Margaret Mary O'Shaughnessy Heckler," *New York Times,* October 3, 1985, II:5.

24. Ibid.

25. Ibid.

Elizabeth Holtzman: Political Reform and Feminist Vision

JOSEPH C. BERTOLINI

Elizabeth Holtzman, the youngest woman ever elected to Congress, is both a pioneer and a flourishing survivor. She has demonstrated during the course of her political career a capacity to sustain a deep commitment to personally held political goals and values and an ability to realize many of them through pragmatic politics. She has been consistent in her political vision but she also has been flexible, blending preferred objectives with an understanding of the constraints imposed by a particular political office or a particular political configuration of power. She has worked tirelessly for women's rights, for decency and honesty in government, for a government that is compassionate and caring, for a legal system that is fair to all, and for many other deeply and sincerely held objectives.

Holtzman always has found public service "extraordinarily challenging and exciting," giving her, she says, "an opportunity to try to improve the quality of life for the community" in which she lives.[1] Her goal has been to change U.S. society and, at the same time, to affirm it. Her commitment, her sincerity, her honesty, her integrity, and her intelligence have never been seriously questioned, even by her opponents.

Throughout her career, regardless of the political office she has occupied, she has maintained a steady vision of a just political community and a constant belief in the need for a government that would right wrongs and redress grievances. Far from being inherently afraid of the power of government, she believes that it can be used positively to counter the hindrances to a decent society. In this sense, she is very much in the Progressive-New Deal-Great Society tradition of using government to rectify social ills and, in the process, to create a little more societal "glue" than was there before. This vision of government has inspired many people in this century to seek political office, Elizabeth Holtzman among them.

Holtzman, however, also has been motivated by a strong sense of personal values, including a commitment to community service and a determination to help the needy and oppressed. Her strong resolve to aid the afflicted through governmental action would seem to be rooted in this deep, ethical, quasi-religious personal imperative, most probably derived from early family, religious, or community experience. She cites the importance of the teachings of the religious philosopher Rabbi Hillel on the development of her thinking. She always has believed, with Hillel, that concern for the self, for the individual, must be balanced by the social demands on the self. She believes that the individual cannot be thought of as isolated from family, community, or neighborhood, that one has a responsibility for others.[2]

Public Service

As a child, Holtzman attended Brooklyn Ethical Culture School, where her strong sense of values was undoubtedly reinforced. She also attended Abraham Lincoln High School and, indicating an early interest in politics, became a leader of the student government. She majored in American history and literature at Radcliffe College and graduated *magna cum laude*. In 1962, long before it was commonplace for women to do so, Holtzman enrolled at Harvard Law School, one of fifteen women in a class of five hundred men. Holtzman was not at all deterred by her minority status and received her law degree in 1965. She interrupted her law studies at one point during this period to spend several months working with a civil rights lawyer in Georgia, where she gained her first real experience with the lives and problems of those who are poor, needy, and discriminated against in the United States. This encounter had a serious impact on her developing political commitment. It increased her determination to do what she could to help these people through the governmental process.

In 1967 Holtzman became a mayoral assistant to New York City Mayor John V. Lindsay. She served as the liaison representative between the mayor's office and the Department of Parks, Recreation, and Cultural Affairs. In this capacity she put special effort into obtaining financial assistance for the city's public library system. She also worked diligently to obtain protective rubber padding for the city's playgrounds.

Although her principal efforts were successful, Holtzman nonetheless found working with the bureaucracy to be quite frustrating. "She objected to the tangles of bureaucratic red tape that delayed or prevented the implementation of necessary public programs."[3] Concerned that the political system was not responding well to human need, she determined to run for public office to make the system work better. In 1970 she was elected Democratic state committeewoman, representing the Flatbush district of Brooklyn, and, in 1972, she decided to run for Congress.

Wanting to prove that government *could* work well and serve the people effectively, she ran in the Democratic primary against Emanuel Celler, who had represented New York's Sixteenth Congressional District since 1922. To Holtzman, Celler seemed to epitomize the very diffident, insensitive, and passé political and bureaucratic leadership that she saw as the cause of the alienation of the citizenry from its government. Celler, she argued, was out of touch. She criticized him for his poor attendance record and his opposition to programs that she considered necessary for the district, "including cost of living increases added to social security benefits, the equal rights amendment to the Constitution and a dozen major aid to education bills."[4] She attacked him for his support of the Vietnam War and his opposition to consumer protection and environmental bills. She accused him of conflicts of interest and of representing special interest groups instead of the people of his district.

Her case against Celler was strongly argued, and her campaign was energetically conducted. She plunged into the race with fervor. She was determined to prove that the people wanted and needed a more responsive, upright government, which she could provide. Her determination paid off. Celler underestimated Holtzman's challenge and did not campaign hard. Holtzman defeated him and then easily defeated her Republican opponent in the predominantly Democratic district. Upon her arrival in the House, Holtzman became the first Democratic woman to serve on the House Budget Committee. She also became chair of the House Judiciary Subcommittee on Immigration, Refugees, and International Law.

Unlike many previous reformers who promised to institute changes upon taking office and then conveniently neglected to do so, Holtzman kept her promise to conduct open, responsive, efficient government. Knowing that many of the nation's citizens, in 1973, felt that their government was not listening to them and not responding to their interests, Holtzman determined to spend half of her time in Washington and the other half in her Brooklyn office connecting directly with her constituents. She also began immediately to advocate specific governmental reforms, arguing, for example, in her initial speech before the House, that proposed new rules of evidence for the federal courts would be too biased in favor of governmental secrecy. Too much information, she held, could be classified as "official" and be withdrawn from legal debate. Holtzman saw this proposed code as the antithesis of open, democratic, responsible government, and so she proposed a bill that would make the code subject to congressional approval. This was her first proposed bill. It passed the House in March 1973 by a 399–1 vote. It also passed in the Senate and on April 1, 1973, it became law.[5] Holtzman was clearly off to a good start. In her first few months as a member of Congress, she had demonstrably kept her promise to provide open, reformist, effective government for her constituents and for the nation.

If Holtzman had kept faith with the U.S. people, however, the Nixon administration, in her judgment, had not. As if to deliberately confirm her analysis of what was wrong with much of contemporary government, the Nixon White House, in her view, engaged in irresponsible governance and massive deception on an apparently unprecedented scale.

In Southeast Asia, beginning in 1969, the Nixon administration, unknown to Congress or the U.S. people, had been engaging in an aerial bombardment of Cambodia. In April 1970, U.S. forces attacked Cambodia in what was termed an "incursion." These actions seemed to stretch the law to the breaking point. In response to this situation, Holtzman originated the first lawsuit that eventually led to the declaration that the bombing of Cambodia was unconstitutional. She also voted against the War Powers Bill of 1973, not because she opposed the intent of the bill—to limit presidential warmaking power—but because she believed that the bill would actually give the president too much leeway in sending troops into combat operations.

Holtzman also clashed with the Nixon White House about the Watergate scandal. As a member of the Judiciary Committee, she developed a reputation as an aggressive questioner during the 1974 impeachment hearings on the president. It was during these sessions that she first came to be generally known by the public. She developed a reputation for stern moral probity, righteous anger, and indignation at the unfolding scandal. She also participated later in the committee's questioning of President Ford about the Nixon pardon.

With the conclusion of U.S. involvement in the Vietnam War and with Nixon's resignation, two egregious examples of governmental irresponsibility and insensitivity, in Holtzman's view, had been brought to an end. There were, of course, many other matters of consequence to address, and she continued to deal with them during her four terms in the House.

Then, in 1980, Holtzman decided to be a candidate for the Senate from New York. She won the Democratic primary handily, becoming, thereby, the first woman in New York to win a major party assignment for the Senate. She was ultimately defeated in November, however, by Republican Alphonse D'Amato in a three-way race that included veteran legislator Jacob Javits as the Liberal party candidate. She lost by approximately 1 percent of some 6 million votes. It could be argued that without Javits in the race she would have been the probable victor.

In 1981 Holtzman ran for district attorney of Kings County (Brooklyn) in New York, one of the largest district attorney's offices in the country. Upon winning election she became the first female district attorney in the history of New York City and the second in New York State. She has always expressed much satisfaction with this position, considering it to be a very exciting and challenging job. She has had to deal with some of the nation's toughest and most intractable problems of government, such as crime and corruption. Holtzman finds the effort to fashion some answers to these problems an exciting challenge. She attests to having found "a lot of room in the position for innovation and experimentation." She believes that she can "develop models for ways of fighting crime that can be useful elsewhere in the nation."[6] Always seeing the broader implications of her work, Holtzman has obviously not ruled out the possibility of seeking higher office. Firming up her base, she ran for and won reelection in 1985.

General Issues

Holtzman has been concerned with many different issues during her career. They can be grouped, however, into several large categories that reflect her concerns and activities throughout her career as a public servant.

Honesty and integrity in government have consistently been two of Holtzman's chief concerns. She always has believed that government is a public trust and that people in government should be honest and above reproach. Governmental service, she would hold, is a privilege, an opportunity to serve the people and strengthen their democratic faith. Such service is an opportunity to do for people what they are unable to do for themselves. Neither venal self-interest nor bureaucratic indifference can be allowed to interfere with this task. Given this perspective, it is not surprising that she would have become so exercised by Watergate or by the Nixon pardon. Further, as a congresswoman, she was noted for exposing fraud in the New York City summer lunch program—an inquiry that led to seventeen convictions. As district attorney she has fought for stronger anticorruption laws, for state laws against influence peddling, for state campaign finance reforms, for legal protection for whistle-blowers who uncover corruption, for the strengthening of the power of state prosecutors, and for more checks on the appointment process in local government.[7] In response to political scandals in New York City in 1986 involving county party leaders, Holtzman suggested that the power of the borough presidents be reduced in order to reduce the opportunity for corruption.

She points to improvements, at the federal level, in many areas after the public exposure that resulted from the Watergate scandal. She notes such reforms as the creation of the special prosecutor's office, the establishment of the federal financial disclosure laws, and the enactment of the campaign finance laws. Holtzman's involvement in the Watergate hearings helped to bring about these reforms. She hopes that similar public attention to these problems on the state level can bring about reforms there also.

Social welfare issues always have been of great concern to Holtzman.

Most of her work in this area was accomplished, of course, when she was in Congress. She worked for such programs as federal aid for low-income housing, federal assistance for local law enforcement, food stamp eligibility for social security recipients, federal aid to education, environmental protection, mass transit aid, and handgun regulation.

She has been particularly concerned with health issues, having done, for example, the first work in Congress on possible dangers from microwave legislation. In 1979 she held hearings on safety problems at the Indian Point nuclear power plant in New York. She also dealt with rather more esoteric health matters such as the failure on the part of drug companies to do sufficient research on drugs for people with rare diseases. They neglected this research because there were few people with these diseases, and the resultant profits would be too low. Holtzman believed this was an area where the federal government could help.[8]

The latter problem is a clear example of Holtzman's belief that government can intervene positively where the free market cannot. It is also an example of her industrious zeal to help those in need, no matter how small a group they may constitute in terms of votes. If government can help and if this help is really necessary, then Holtzman wants government to act. She seems to believe sincerely that if there is a problem that cannot be resolved by the free market, then there must be a bill that she can propose to resolve it. Holtzman proposed many such bills when she was in Congress, a highly respectable proportion of which were enacted. Overall, she has been an effective legislator.

War and peace issues always have assumed a paramount position in Holtzman's hierarchy of concerns. The Vietnam War, a conflict she very much opposed, was most certainly a prime reason for her involvement in national politics in the first place.[9] Her aforementioned, notable legal action against the U.S. incursion into Cambodia was an extension of this same concern.

Holtzman's interest in efforts at international peace and cooperation is today as strong as ever, although as Brooklyn district attorney her duties are of an essentially local nature. Nonetheless, whenever possible, she continues to speak out on such issues as the need for a nuclear testing moratorium and a nuclear freeze. She believes both to be very much needed.[10] Her concern with foreign policy matters thus remains unabated.

Crime control in general is a constant Holtzman theme. Those who break the law, she holds, should be punished, whether the perpetrator is the president of the United States, a car thief in Brooklyn, or a Nazi war criminal. She is consistently relentless and aggressive in pursuit of criminals, believing that vigorous law enforcement can make a difference.

Her approach to law enforcement is another example of how committed Holtzman is to the rule of law and to the use of law to remedy social ills.

This is, of course, a belief particular to this country and one that is most probably reinforced by her legal training and her essentially liberal perspective. Naturally, if laws are to be used to solve problems, then it logically follows that they must be enforced in order to be effective.

In Congress Holtzman investigated everything from presidential illegalities to summer lunch program fraud. She was a co-sponsor of the Crime Control Act of 1976, and she worked on legislation to compensate crime victims and regulate handguns. She also developed a special interest in working against Nazi war criminals living in the United States. She was the first member of Congress to expose government inaction against suspected Nazi war criminals. She forced the Justice Department to create a special unit to investigate them and wrote the law that authorized their deportation from the country. She has pursued international lawbreakers as determinedly as domestic ones.

Holtzman's anticrime crusade has been very effective in Brooklyn. During her tenure as district attorney, her office has achieved a very high conviction rate, the highest in New York City in 1983. She also implemented numerous measures to help crime victims. She has embraced her crime-fighting duties with gusto and with a sense of mission. For example, before she took office, auto theft had become virtually decriminalized in Brooklyn, and, hence, it was increasing constantly. Prosecutors acted as if the problem were insoluble and inevitably would get worse, so strenuous efforts on their part to eliminate or reduce it would be, in their view, pointless. Holtzman would have none of this. She chose to aggressively attack the problem. As a result of her strong approach, there were more arrests, more indictments, more convictions, and tougher sentences meted out than before. She treated auto theft as a real felony and put people in jail. As a result, she accomplished a 20 percent boroughwide reduction in the crime. She proudly refers to her success in this area as an example of what honest, assertive, positive government can accomplish.

Discrimination is another issue that has always been of particular importance to Holtzman. As a young civil rights worker in the South she worked to end racial discrimination. In Congress she worked to eliminate social security discrimination against working widows. She also drafted the first bill that provided criminal penalties for discrimination in employment. As district attorney, she has sought remedies to the problem of racial discrimination in jury selection.

Holtzman has always believed in the theoretical goal written into the Declaration of Independence that people should be treated equally. She subscribes also to the updated version of this idea—that people should be treated equally regardless of sex, age, race, or anything else. Discrimination, she argues, prevents people from realizing their own potential. Hence, government is needed to ensure that the individual's basic rights are not contravened. Government can help the individual to become a full individual by "hindering the hindrances" to the full development of the self.

Women's Issues

Discrimination against women and women's issues in general are of special interest to Holtzman. In Congress she was very outspoken on feminist concerns. A strong advocate of the Equal Rights Amendment, she authored the law that extended the deadline for its ratification. She also wrote and pushed through Congress laws that protected the privacy of rape victims in federal trials and made pornography a federal crime. She wrote legislation that was enacted "to allow the recovery of attorney's fees in Title IX discrimination cases, to make it a crime to discriminate against women in Federal public works projects, to prohibit the State Department from helping foreign governments or businesses to enter into contracts with U.S. concerns that discriminate against women, and to prevent sex discrimination in refugee resettlement programs." She also introduced legislation to ban child pornography, "to ensure that women are not denied benefits when their husbands die before retirement age, to guarantee that men may not decide unilaterally to deny their wives survivor's benefits and to ensure that benefit levels for a woman who survives her husband are adequate."[11]

Believing that strength lies in unity and that women should organize and work together, Holtzman co-founded the first congresswoman's caucus and was elected first Democratic chair of that bipartisan group. She always has held that women's issues can cut across party lines, that women as women must work together for common goals if they are going to be attained at all.

As King's County district attorney, Holtzman has continued to make women's issues a prime concern. She led successful campaigns to amend New York State laws to remove serious obstacles to the prosecution of rapists and child molesters. She eliminated discrimination against women in her own office.[12] Further, acting upon complaints from women that they were being discriminated against in the New York State court system, Holtzman pressed for the establishment of a statewide Task Force on Women in the Courts. This investigative body uncovered a scandalously large amount of prejudicial conduct on the part of male judges and attorneys toward female attorneys and witnesses.[13] Upon release of the report, Holtzman pushed for reforms to discipline and reprimand the perpetrators of these prejudicial, demeaning, discriminatory actions.

Ultimately, however, Holtzman believes that women will not really achieve full equality of opportunity until there are "more women in positions of power in this country, whether in elected or appointed positions."

She believes that unless "women are in that capacity, it's going to take a lot longer to make the changes that are necessary."[14] Holtzman wants women to register and then to vote and elect women into political office. She believes that only by "voting [can] women compel the government to do what it is unwilling to do on its own."[15] She argues that only women can really motivate the political system to transcend its natural bureaucratic inertia and enact laws that will promote equality for women. Here she is well within the standard U.S. tradition of interest group politics.

Holtzman also believes, however, that, inevitably the true, full liberation of women to a position of genuine equality will fully liberate *all* of U.S. society. She holds that the women's movement should not be thought of only as the project of a particular interest group but, instead, as a vehicle for broader change. Feminism is a movement for human dignity, for human equality. It is not just concerned with female interests. As such, it has the power to change the world, as did the American and French revolutions. Just as these revolutions, these movements, she attests, began in particular countries and with particular groups and then overflowed to change the world, so, also, will feminism overflow and become a general drive for human liberation. The women's movement stirs deep emotions of freedom and equality, emotions that are endemic to the human spirit. They cannot be stirred and then placed back in the bottle again or restricted to a particular country or a particular group of people. There might be roadblocks or detours, but, in the end, Holtzman is certain that freedom will triumph. Inevitably, women will have true equality in the United States and their attainment will be an example to women worldwide. Eventually, women will be fully free and this will help to fully humanize both women *and* men.

Holtzman, then, believes (echoing Elizabeth Cady Stanton) that the "true woman," the fully equal woman, can become a critical "force for good" in the world. She believes that the "true woman" is "integral to a decent moral order," that she can be a "force for peace, for justice, for ending the spectre of poverty, illiteracy, and joblessness." In this sense, feminism becomes, for Holtzman, a vehicle for world change of a virtually revolutionary nature. Women, she is convinced, "can transform the world." All that it will take is "the will to do so."[16] Besides, history is on the side of feminism, just as it was on the side of the American and French revolutions. Humanistic, basic change is coming that will essentially reshape the social order and address the world's ills in a fundamental manner unlike anything that has come before. Women, potentially, have the power to change the world's ethical perspective and thereby change the way the world's most intractable problems are comprehended. A movement for freedom, then, generated by half the world's population could free the whole world by bringing women's deepest and best abilities to bear on our most intransigent difficulties and by effecting fundamental ethical change in the primary human relationship, that between a man and a woman.

Conclusion

Holtzman's honesty, integrity, sincerity, and commitment are her most impressive qualities. She would appear to be wholly incorruptible. She most certainly is sincere in what she says, and she really believes in her vision of a better world. She is a zealous reformer and a visionary. In addition, she has been an extremely effective politician, highly adept at turning her desires and beliefs into legislative realities on both the federal and state levels. She also has been an aggressive and effective district attorney, vigorously pursuing lawbreakers. In effect, she has plunged thoroughly into every job that she has had, working assiduously and determinedly to use her position as a vehicle for reform. She has enormous faith in the basic soundness and potential of the political system, in the power of human will, in her optimistic vision of the future, and in her ethical conception of individual-social relations. She never seems to be discouraged, and she never seems to be tired or world-weary.

However, the tempering, moderating effect of a degree of world-weariness, of doubt, has a positive value for any reformer, Holtzman included. Holtzman is perhaps too quick to assume that truly complex problems can be really resolved primarily by passing laws, that persistent social ills, perhaps endemic to a given culture or a given sociopolitical system, are remediable through legislation. Besides, there is a certain tragic dimension to the human experience, often neglected by U.S. optimism, that no law can dispel. Reforms, too, have a way of creating new problems, often previously unforeseen. In the end, there is only so much that is subject to human will.

Holtzman, however, would most probably argue that if we don't try to solve our problems, particularly the most recalcitrant ones, how can there be even the chance of improvement? Some progress, she would hold, is better than none at all. This is surely a telling point. Politicians, in the final analysis, are not philosophers. Politicians must act—they must try. Above all else, Holtzman has tried.

Notes

1. Elizabeth Holtzman, quoted in Julie Clifford and John Hanson, "Elizabeth Holtzman: New York City's First Woman District Attorney," *American Politics* (January 1984):12–13.

2. Elizabeth Holtzman, personal interview with Joseph C. Bertolini, May 5, 1986.

3. "Holtzman, Elizabeth," *Current Biography* (New York: H. W. Wilson, 1973), 191.

4. Ibid.

5. Ibid., 192.

6. Holtzman in Clifford, "Elizabeth Holtzman," 13.

7. Elizabeth Holtzman, "New York State Needs Stronger Anti-Corruption Laws," *New York Times,* February 22, 1986, 23.

8. Holtzman, interview.

9. Ibid.

10. Ibid.

11. Elizabeth Holtzman, "Women's Rights," *Congressional Record* vol. 126, Part 25 (December 30, 1980):34427–34429.

12. Elizabeth Holtzman, "Comment: It's Better Being Boss," *Working Woman* (January 1983), 40.

13. Jeffrey Schmalz, "Pervasive Sex Bias Found in Courts," *New York Times,* April 20, 1986, 1, 40.

14. Holtzman, "Comment."

15. Elizabeth Holtzman, "Viewpoints: Fearful Men Beat the ERA," *Newsday,* November 30, 1983, 59.

16. Elizabeth Holtzman, "Through Their Struggle for Equality, Women Can Create A More Humanitarian Society," *Radcliffe Quarterly* (September 1983), 5.

J

Nancy Landon Kassebaum: From School Board to Senate

LINDA K. RICHTER

"Well Toto, something tells me we're not in Kansas." As laughter spread through the National Press Club, Senator Nancy Landon Kassebaum continued her speech, mixing a characteristically gentle humor with tough appraisals of the political agenda awaiting congressional action. This "Dorothy" held her own that day in the political "Oz" that is Washington, D.C.[1] The speech was vintage Kassebaum. The junior senator from Kansas, known in Washington as "nice little Nancy" when first elected senator in 1978, has learned to move attention beyond her petite figure and pleasant demeanor to an appreciation of her candor and reasonableness in a city more known for political intrigue and grandstanding.

When Nancy Kassebaum became the first woman in U.S. history elected senator who had not followed her husband into politics, there was widespread expectation in Washington that she would be a political lightweight. A full-time homemaker for twenty-one years, mother of four, separated (and later divorced) from Philip Kassebaum, a wealthy Wichita lawyer, she scarcely fit the image of a successful senator—especially when the other ninety-nine were male! Her only previous electoral success was as member of the school board of the small town, Maize, Kansas. Even many of her supporters feared she had moved too abruptly from homemaker to politician; her critics complained that she had not earned such a candidacy by running for lesser political offices in the state or in the Republican party. But there were many clues in her background that could have predicted such a candidacy had she been male, and in many respects she shares a similar political background with other successful women candidates.

Kassebaum came from a home in which politics was the staple of conversation all her life. She was little more than a toddler in 1936 when her father, Alf Landon, then governor of Kansas, ran for the presidency against incumbent Franklin Roosevelt. The thorough drubbing he received (he carried only two states) discouraged further electoral bids, but the Landon home remained for more than fifty years a center of debate and discussion of Kansas and national politics. Even when banished from adult conversations, Nancy in her room above the library would listen to the discussions through the heating vents!

As an adult, Kassebaum continued her interest in politics, and her education was comparable to others who entered politics. She received a B.A. in political science from the University of Kansas and an M.A. in diplomatic history from the University of Michigan. Although she initially prepared for a Foreign Service career, like many women of her generation those plans were set aside when she decided to marry. Her husband became a lawyer and later a prominent businessman in Wichita. She became a homemaker, active in community and school affairs. In tiny Maize, Kansas (near Wichita) she is remembered for having tutored children, started the school library, and participated in a host of other civic activities.

Kassebaum's decision to pursue a political career was deferred until her children were adolescents. In fact, Senator Kassebaum always has contended that her family was her number one priority and that had her marriage remained intact she would not have considered running for an elected office. Nevertheless, she acknowledges that there have been some outstanding political women who have combined family and political lives successfully, such as Carla Hills, President Ford's housing and urban development secretary, and Supreme Court Justice Sandra Day O'Connor. Still, the average politically active woman becomes involved in electoral politics in her forties, about ten years later than do men. Thus, she consciously or unconsciously escapes some of the criticism younger political women encounter—namely, that they are "neglecting" their "primary" role as homemakers. As a consequence of later entry into public life, most women in politics never acquire the seniority and experience to move into key leadership roles in government. Senator Kassebaum's late start fits this pattern, but her unusual step in running directly for the U.S. Senate without intermediate campaigns at the local or state level meant that she entered that body no older than most male freshman senators.

The decision to run for the U.S. Senate was a fortuitous and unexpected opportunity. After her separation in 1975, Kassebaum took her three younger children to Washington, D.C. where she had planned to work for the State Department. Senator James Pearson, then senior senator from Kansas, prevailed upon her to work for him instead. That experience proved extremely valuable in preparing Kassebaum for the realities of congressional life, particularly the importance of able staff and good office organization.

She returned to Kansas with her children a year later, where friends encouraged her to run for office in the 1978 elections. Initially, she considered running for the Fifth District House of Representatives seat, but although technically living in that district, she felt closer to the political life of nearby Wichita. When Senator James Pearson decided to retire in 1978, the GOP Senate race was suddenly wide open. Several people announced their candidacy, including Jan Meyers, one of two women then serving in the Kansas Senate.[2] At first, Kassebaum wondered if she should run against another woman. "But then I thought, no man would back down from a candidacy because another man was running." That settled, Nancy Landon Kassebaum became one of the nine GOP candidates for the U.S. Senate.

The timing was right. Her children were old enough, her family responsibilities diminished. She was wealthy, and the Landon name still spelled magic in Kansas Republican politics. Despite the fact that the Who's Who of Kansas Republican politics had known Nancy since childhood, Kassebaum did have some fund-raising problems in the primary. The party was officially neutral. Her late entry into the race also foreclosed some funding sources, and her own unwillingness to accept contributions of more than $1,000 from political action committees meant she had to reach beyond her political contacts for her campaign. Friends from her undergraduate days at the University of Kansas proved loyal and generous.

Family support for a female candidate has usually been found to be a much more important variable for women than men. She had this support from her husband, who though separated remained a close confidant, her mother, and her mother-in-law.[3] She especially treasures the enthusiasm her mother showed for her candidacy because Theo Landon's own life has been an apolitical, traditional one. Her father, Alf Landon, was not so thrilled. "Of course now he's a great fan and loves having a senator in the family, but then he was certain I'd lose." When it was suggested he might have sought to dissuade her because he wanted to protect her from heartbreak, she cheerfully rejected that interpretation. "I think he was more afraid that I'd embarrass him." He came around, however, and by the eve of her announcement of candidacy he was brainstorming with her about questions she could expect from the press. "My views on abortion will be a sure topic," she noted. "Abortion!" he exclaimed. "What business does the press or the government have in getting into a private matter like that!"

The Campaign

Abortion was an issue, however. Because Kassebaum maintained that such an option should remain legal and up to the individual, her campaign attracted the wrath of many who favored prohibiting abortion. Everywhere she campaigned she and/or her children were met with signs, "Nancy Kills Babies" or "Nancy Murders Unborn." Although the placards dismayed her, she said they reinforced her feeling that no group should make such a personal decision for another.

Throughout the campaign she resisted mentioning abortion, the ERA, or women's rights unless specifically asked, for she feared that her candidacy might be perceived too narrowly. Nor would she make political promises to specific interest groups. She felt that such special interest politics were a part of the problem, not the solution.

Her rivals attempted to focus on her lack of a track record in politics, but her own campaign diffused the issue by concentrating on a large and very positive media campaign (which she could afford) that featured her talking with her popular father, speaking before male audiences, and discussing inflation from her kitchen counter or while bringing in groceries. In the first advertisement she reinforced the association with the positive "Landon" name. In the second she implied she could hold her own with men, and in the home scene she conveyed a nonthreatening image as a thoughtful homemaker.

Her very size invited disdain, however. One commentator referred to her as a "wounded wren"—scarcely an image of power and competence![4] Such comments on physique were not directed at the other candidates. Her foundering marriage was also a latent issue, although Senator Robert Dole's divorce and remarriage had attracted little attention a few years earlier.

In what was a preview of the obsessive concern shown for Geraldine Ferraro's spouse and his business dealings in the 1984 election, Kassebaum was hounded by the press to force her estranged husband to release his tax returns. Kassebaum said that she could thoroughly empathize with Ferraro during the 1984 election and that a double standard was applied to female candidates for high office. She stuck to her decision not to release her husband's tax statement, and the fact that they were separated perhaps kept the issue from remaining a damaging one.

Despite the obstacles, Kassebaum won the primary handily and went on to defeat three-term Democratic congressman Bill Roy in the general election. She won without the endorsement of key women's organizations, which supported Roy, but with the edge provided by the Landon name, a Republican majority among the state's registered voters, and the funds that could buy good media coverage and competent campaign assistance. Her credentials established, by 1984 Nancy Kassebaum was the overwhelming favorite for reelection. The only real question on the Democratic side was who would be the sacrificial lamb to run against the popular incumbent.

In Office

Once in office, Kassebaum sought and received a position on the important Committee on Commerce, Science, and Transportation where she served on the Aviation Subcommittee. By 1980 she was the subcommittee chairwoman—a position of considerable importance to constituents in and around Wichita, the state's largest city and a major defense and civilian aircraft building center. She also served on the Budget Committee, a relatively new committee but one with growing prestige and saliency.

Within two years she had a highly coveted seat on the Senate Foreign Relations Committee, from which she could put to use her extensive background in U.S. diplomatic history. She would later become chairwoman of the African Affairs Subcommittee. She also was appointed to a position on the Select Committee on Ethics. Each of these committee appointments offered unusual leadership opportunities for a new senator. Kassebaum acknowledges that she was incredibly lucky, for in 1980 the Republicans gained control of the Senate for the first time since 1954, which enabled her to assume leadership of key subcommittees.

Despite good committee assignments and Republican successes, Senator Kassebaum's political career had added pressures as well. She divorced, although the lengthy separation made the actual divorce a nonissue politically. Second, despite her eagerness to be considered a senator in the generic sense of the term, being the only female in a very traditional "old boys' club" made that impossible. She was an immediate novelty for the press, for the lecture circuit, and for all manner of clubs and organizations. Interview and speaking requests soared even as her political decisions and work received unusual scrutiny. It was the familiar dilemma of the "token." Like it or not, she was considered a representative of women as well as of Kansas. Nor did the election of Florida Republican Senator Paula Hawkins in 1980 lessen Kassebaum's responsibilities appreciably because Hawkins' politics was decidedly more conservative and politically less palatable to major women's organizations.

The Republican party was intrigued with its popular senator, but it took awhile for the party to appreciate her substantive abilities. Even in 1980 the state GOP convention introduced her to the tune of "Ain't She Sweet"! At one national-level strategy session on how to combat the gender gap and make the party more attractive to females, no one even thought to ask the Republican women officeholders for their opinion. At last, "nice little Nancy" pointed that out. Kassebaum's awareness of her status as the lone female in the Senate (in 1978) was heightened by the attitude of many of her fellow senators. There initially was a certain condescension that was not helped at all by her first speech on the Senate floor. In keeping with her campaign speeches extolling turnover of politicians, her "maiden" speech called for a two-term limit for senators. One could scarcely imagine a topic less likely to endear the lone female to her colleagues or one more apt to convince them of her naïveté. Seven years' experience in office has not only brought that self-imposed deadline closer to the senator, but it has honed her political instincts.

While still insisting that turnover is desirable and healthy, Kassebaum says she has seen the "lame duck" phenomenon firsthand and wants to avoid it herself. Citing Majority Leader Howard Baker's reduced effectiveness once he'd announced he would not seek reelection and even Ronald Reagan's reduced clout in his second term, she now will not rule out a third term. Kassebaum insists that she is keeping her options open. This way she retains her power and her political flexibility.

Today, the senator is considered a bellwether vote on many issues because of her thoughtful, moderate, nonideological stance. Bipartisan agreement, consistent policies, and genuine compromise measures appear to be her trademarks, although she insists that her efforts are less manipulative than they are a genuine reflection of her middle-of-the-road views.

Although Kassebaum exhibits a more benign and gentle posture than her Kansas colleague, Senator Dole, whose caustic wit is legendary, her voting record reflects a significant independence from White House views on a variety of issues ranging from the MX missile, the ERA, apartheid, population planning, and presidential appointments. Her differences with the president's position are never couched in strident rhetoric, and her interpretations of Reagan's positions are always generous, but she makes no secret of her feeling that slavish adherence to one's party or one's president may mean a more serious disloyalty to oneself. For example, when asked in interviews about her interest in becoming a vice presidential candidate she assured questioners she would not be coy about her aspirations should she decide she wants to be nominated. A more important question for her is how compatible her views would be with those of a presidential candidate and how much diversity each could tolerate. She implied that the example of George Bush's subordination of his own views to a defense of the president's very different positions would have been intolerable for her.

To Nancy Kassebaum at least part of the difference between her attitude and that of many of the political men around her lies in the very different socialization of the sexes to politics. To women, she feels, politics is not an all-consuming obsession; there are other important facets of life beyond the political struggle. Men, on the other hand, generally see the political contest and the jockeying for political power as more critical. The stakes seem higher, the outcomes more central to their sense of esteem. This, she suggests, does not make men better at politics. It only means that they conceptualize politics differently and commit more of their egos to it.

Moderate With a Cause

One of the attractions of following Nancy Landon Kassebaum's political career—and one of the irritations—is that she, like her father before her, defies pigeonholing. In general, she's conservative fiscally, liberal on some domestic social issues, conservative on others, a frugal internationalist, a moderate feminist, and a careful student of her constituents' interests. She tries not to tilt at windmills (and with the exception of her first Senate speech has largely avoided doing so). She has sometimes carried this unwillingness to posture a bit far, refusing to support largely symbolic gestures and thereby offending certain groups without reaping any political benefits from her independent stand. At other times, the fact that she decides each issue pragmatically has added to her influence in the Senate. It means that senators and interest groups across the entire political spectrum, not simply conservatives or Republicans, seek her votes, and she retains access to them when issues close to her are before the Senate. She is not automatically in anyone's camp, including the Reagan administration's.

General Issues

The gun control issue is a good example. Almost no senator is eager to take on the powerful National Rifle Association, but if one is so audacious, the safest step is to seek support from the smaller but still active gun control groups. Kassebaum instead went right down the middle, refusing to suspend her judgment on the issue merely because the topic had become polarized. As usual she was seeking a viable compromise that would save "face" for both sides and save U.S. lives. "Gun control has become an extremely emotional issue. Gun enthusiasts seem to feel that any government restraint at all will inevitably lead to total control and confiscation of all firearms. Gun control supporters, on the other hand, show little understanding of responsible individuals who want to own guns for legitimate sporting, collecting, and defense purposes. Neither perspective is complete."[5]

Nor does a previous stand on a particular issue mean she will routinely continue to oppose or support that position. The MX missile is a good example. Kassebaum initially supported the controversial weapons program because she felt the missile's greater accuracy and mobile basing system represented a decided advance over the intercontinental ballistic missiles (ICBMs) based in their fixed silos. As the issue was rehashed and reformulated, the number of missiles was reduced, and to save costs the missiles were to be installed in the old ICBM fixed silos. Kassebaum rejected the new packaging and voted against the MX system. Although in favor of budget cuts, Kassebaum felt that putting a sharply reduced sophisticated system in the old vulnerable silos destroyed the entire logic of having the MX, thereby making the entire investment unwise. The MX also had not sparked any arms control talks with the Soviets, as the Reagan administration had argued it would. So she changed her mind.[6]

Kassebaum rejects attempts to define national security only in terms of the military budget or hardware. National security considerations were involved in her decision to support the Panama Canal Treaty—a vote deemed treasonous by the radical right in her own party and the then-presidential candidate, Ronald Reagan.

Long-range foreign policy considerations also were involved in her policy positions vis-à-vis Africa and Central America. For a long time she supported the president's policy of not imposing economic sanctions on South Africa because she was not convinced they would be effective. But she broke with that position months before the president partially abandoned it, realizing that the situation demanded an active U.S. response if only to retain influence elsewhere in Africa.

Kassebaum also has fought the president on military spending in El Salvador, where she feels such monies have often been misplaced. The *Washington Post* and moderates in both parties have applauded her insistence on the necessity of negotiation in that conflict.[7] She has chided her party's support of anticommunist dictators and lack of support for the democratic processes in such countries that could weaken the appeal of communism.

> If a government that claims our friendship cannot sustain the support of its own people, or as too often seems to happen, is actively involved in repressing its own people, then there is little we can do over the long run to defend them. Such governments are their own worst enemies, and we delude both them and ourselves to think that American money, arms, and men can be a substitute for the support of their own people.
>
> There is a basic principle here that our party and our nation should take to heart. For too long, we have judged our friends only by their rhetoric on Marxism. If we want to protect our own interests, then we must also protect the basic values on which those interests are founded. In short, we should expect our friends not merely to oppose Communism, but to actively promote democracy within their own borders—for their good and ours.
>
> This is not a matter of being sentimental about the glories of democracy. It is a matter of being realistic about the powerful appeal of change, particularly in nations where the status quo is both brutal and bleak.[8]

Similarly, her positions with respect to hunger in Africa go well beyond shipment of surplus Kansas foodstuffs. She has called for fundamental reorganization of food production and international development bureaucracies. With respect to both she is a partisan of decentralization and small-scale projects.[9]

In addition to her experience as chair of the African Affairs Subcommittee, Kassebaum also has been influenced by the Peace Corps work in Togo of her daughter Linda. There even small projects became bogged down in layers of administration and forms. Too often tiny but practical and vital programs get overlooked in the process. One such women's program—a tomato-processing factory that meant economic independence for dozens of women in that area—was saved by the senator's intervention. Women's work and women's needs can be easily overlooked in the overwhelmingly male bureaucracies of both donor and recipient nations.

Bureaucracy and cost effectiveness, not isolationism, were at issue in the senator's call for reducing the U.S. financial commitment to the United Nations. Unlike many who supported this Kassebaum amendment because they resented the loss of U.S. control in that body and the rising power of Third World nations, Kassebaum's primary complaint was economic. She argued that the U.N. wages were far above those of the public sector in the U.S. or any other member nation, that staffing was excessive, and that administration was generally sloppy. Her amendment, she contended, would not hurt worthwhile programs but would make overall administration more cost effective.[10]

Senatorial procedures are not immune to Kassebaum's scrutiny. The process of arguing the MX and other issues again and again at several stages in the policy process persuaded her that the debates on authorization of funds and appropriations should be merged. This, she feels, would reduce unnecessary rhetoric at the authorization stage, focus attention on the overall policy, and help determine realistically how much money should actually be spent for it. She also supports a two-year budget cycle and modifications of the Senate filibuster rules.

Kassebaum is unusual in her attention to such process concerns. Monitoring performance and procedure is critically important, but it is not an activity legislators or even the administration readily embraces, for the political dividends are few. However, it may have contributed to her selection as chairwoman of the 1980 and deputy chairwoman of the 1984 Republican conventions.

Her attention to process and detail should not obscure the fact that her general inclination is to be a team player. When she can't agree she tries to make her areas of disagreement clear without attacking others. The Gramm-Rudman Budget Bill of 1985 was a case in point. She felt the bill had serious procedural deficiencies that would undermine its effectiveness but knew that symbolically a budget bill was popular. She voted against the bill and in doing so went against the wishes of the Reagan administration. Within months the bill was under attack in Congress and the courts because of arguments not unlike hers. She also is well known for her ability to build a consensus across party lines. As a moderate Republican her ability to work with Democrats has been extremely important in blunting the legislative thrusts of those in the radical right of her party and the extreme left of the Democratic party.

Women's Issues

One of the arguments advanced for the election of more women to Congress and other positions of influence is that a representative government should reflect in both composition and attitudes the diversity of the society at large. Two interests are at stake here: the constituents' perception that they are represented by people like themselves and the actual representation of the interests of all types of people. We cannot predict, on the basis of sex, how a congresswoman will decide a measure. Even though women make up a small percentage (4 percent) of the Senate and the House membership, a wide variation in viewpoints exists. However, with such a small number of women, there is a clear expectation among the electorate that these women will be involved with and have opinions about issues of significance to women. Thus, although many congresswomen entered Congress intending simply to be members of Congress and not advocates for women, most have discovered that if they aren't such advocates those concerns will not get debated. Moreover, their own marginality in the power structure sensitizes them (however successful they are) to institutionalized sexism. This was also the experience of Nancy Kassebaum. What follows is both a record of her own perception of her role vis-à-vis women and her position on many of the key issues of concern to women.

Kassebaum's position as a feminist supporter of the ERA and pro-choice on the issue of abortion *and* a Republican senator when the popular Republican president is opposed to both positions can't be easy. Add to that the fact that major women's groups in Kansas opposed the first woman senator from Kansas in her initial electoral bid and failed to endorse her reelection bid and it is reasonable to expect that Kassebaum would feel no special need to court this group. Yet on many issues of concern to feminists Kassebaum has supported feminists even when it meant breaking with the Reagan administration. Her recent support of the Civil Rights Restoration Act, which would once more make sex and race discrimination anywhere in an educational institution grounds for cutting off federal funds to that institution, is such an example.

Her initial campaign contained the seeds of her later relationship with women's groups and their issues. First, she chose to define women's issues broadly, as major public issues of fairness, equity, the economy, and national security.

She spoke out against the unfairness of veterans being given a lifetime advantage in hiring because it has become a major obstacle to female employment. Since few women are veterans, they are repeatedly passed over by veterans for jobs even when the women score higher on employment tests. Her opponent supported the continuation of such absolute preferential hiring. While she was courageous in attacking veterans' preference her valor was not appreciated nor her concern understood; the devastating impact of veterans preference on female employment was not widely known at the time—even in feminist organizations—and it infuriated veterans groups.

Similarly, her subtlety in distinguishing between her support for the ERA and her objection to the procedure by which Congress granted an extension in time for ratifying the amendment was largely lost on organizations like the National Organization for Women (NOW) and the Kansas Women's Political Caucus. Any qualification of support for the ERA was heresy to groups that had organized around and fought for the ERA as the symbol and the legal ammunition with which to combat sex discrimination. Her 1978 challenger, Bill Roy, vowed enduring support for the amendment. Second, most of those who thought as she did on women's rights were Democrats. Certainly, many who heard her debate Bill Roy and applauded the idea of a female candidacy already had worked on Roy's earlier winning campaigns for the House of Representatives. Then as now Kassebaum lacked a critical mass of female support from within her own party.

Once elected, Kassebaum joined the Women's Congressional Caucus but has not been active in recent years. The only other female Republican senator, Paula Hawkins, did not join. Kassebaum is dubious about the rapid proliferation of caucuses generally and has remained aloof from all but a few. She did prefer the women's caucus when it was smaller and all female, but she acknowledges that the men who have joined have been important supporters of women's rights. She feels that in recent years the caucus has undertaken sponsorship of some issues, such as unisex insurance rates, without "getting their act together first" and lost in credibility as a result. Although she did not cite the caucus's partisanship as a reason for her own lack of involvement, research has shown that because of its overwhelmingly Democratic majority the caucus has sometimes found it difficult to function as a truly bipartisan body.

Two issues that have separated Kassebaum from many feminists have been her positions on registration for the draft and on comparable worth. On the question of draft registration, Kassebaum fought for the registration of both men and women as consistent with the notion that each sex is legally equal in all obligations of citizenship. Many feminists opposed to registration did not see equal jeopardy as meeting their goals for equal rights. Other feminists contended that until women are guaranteed equality in the Constitution, that is, through the ERA, they shouldn't need to register. Kassebaum would argue that demands for equal rights would carry more weight if women were equally eligible for national service. Even those who disagreed could scarcely argue with the fact that in sponsoring the registration of both men and women Kassebaum was taking equality of rights to its logical conclusion—equality of responsibilities.

On the issue of comparable worth Kassebaum has not quarreled with the severity of the problem of depressed wages for women or the imperfections of the free market, but with the feasibility of developing genuinely reliable indicators of job worth and of utilizing job evaluations in conjunction with a market economy.

> Comparable worth is an attempt to bring order to our very messy, and sometimes unfair, marketplace. It tries to superimpose the social value of fairness over the less human value of economics. Such a goal is understandable, even laudable—if it worked. I don't think it can....
>
> It seems to me that rather than fighting the market, we should be taking steps to promote positive market adjustments. I don't know that the answer is to raise pay for some jobs as they now stand so much as it is to work toward making these jobs building blocks, not dead ends....
>
> One positive aspect of the comparable worth debate is the attention it has drawn to the economic concerns of women. Whether they agree or disagree with the concept, people are taking a much closer look at occupational segregation and discrimination.[11]

Conclusion

If she has not proved to be a perfect heroine of feminist causes, Kassebaum has established herself as a thoughtful and selective supporter of women's rights in the face of little support or encouragement from her own political party. In an era when climbing on the conservative Reagan bandwagon is a popular and politically advantageous move, Kassebaum has earned the bipartisan respect of her colleagues by her independence of thought, her moderate approach to political problems, and her refusal to be seduced by popular and simplistic answers to difficult policy questions.

> I do not doubt the sincerity or motives of those who support these particular points of view. Surely, their advocacy efforts play an important role in focusing attention on serious problems. However, absolute "rightness" just may be a luxury none of us can ever obtain. The ERA may neither provide a panacea for women nor produce the downfall of the family that some expect. School prayer will not restore stability to public schools and family life, but it probably would not lead to religious tyranny either. Our hopes for peace might not be fulfilled by the MX and Star Wars—or by the nuclear freeze and disarmament.
>
> Somewhere between the extremes of each issue lies an answer achieved through the thoughtful negotiation, debate, and compromise that democracy demands.[12]

When asked her top priority as a senator, Kassebaum answered not in terms of legislation, policy sectors, or personal ambition but in terms of her preoccupation with the democratic process. "I want to get people involved in participating in politics. That's why I love to speak to classes—especially elementary schools. If they can get interested when they're young, maybe they'll get involved later."

Nancy Landon Kassebaum may be most important as a female leader, not for her votes or for the legislation she has sponsored or even for the integrity and thoughtfulness of her positions on public issues, but for the role model she provides post-Watergate generations of commitment to the democratic process and involved citizenship.

Notes

1. This chapter is based on a personal interview with Senator Kassebaum on December 6, 1985, and on subsequent phone conversations. I have known the senator since 1981 and have followed her political career since 1978 when I was working for one of her GOP rivals! The senator's staff has made available copies of her speeches, and my own assistant, Angela Pearl, has done much of the tracking of the senator's senatorial votes.

2. Jan Meyers was herself elected to the House of Representatives in 1984 and is running for re-election again in 1986.

3. The importance of family and particularly spouse support has been cited by many scholars. This has been documented in Ruth B. Mandel, *In the Running,* New York, Ticknor and Fields, 1981.

4. "Kansas 'Citizen' Senator Passes Political Muster," *Wall Street Journal,* September 26, 1984.

5. Nancy L. Kassebaum, "Firearm Freedom or Folly" (A speech given July 1985).

6. Nancy L. Kassebaum, "It's Time to Judge MX on Its Own Merits" (A speech given March 1985).

7. "The Kassebaum Formula," *Washington Post,* March 23, 1983, A24.

8. Nancy L. Kassebaum, "The Future of the Republican Party" (A speech given to the National Federation of Republican Women in Phoenix, Arizona, September 21, 1985).

9. Nancy L. Kassebaum, A speech before the Society for International Development, Washington, D.C., June 18, 1985.

10. "Bucking the UN," editorial, *Houston Post,* September 3, 1985.

11. Nancy L. Kassebaum, "The Merits and Demerits of a Comparable Worth System" (A speech given at Notre Dame Law School, February 11, 1985).

12. Nancy L. Kassebaum, A speech given to Alpha Omicron Pi, Washington, D.C., June 28, 1985.

Jeane Kirkpatrick: From the University to the United Nations

NAOMI B. LYNN

In an interview in April 1985 Jeane Kirkpatrick reflected on her recent experience as U.S. Ambassador to the United Nations and as a member of the Reagan cabinet. "I was the only woman in our history, I think, who ever sat in regularly at top-level foreign policy-making meetings. Those arenas have always been closed to women, not only here but in most other countries. And it matters a great deal. It's terribly important, maybe even to the future of the world, for women to take part in making the decisions that shape our destiny."[1]

Jeane Jordan Kirkpatrick was a respected political scientist, a professor at Georgetown University, and a resident scholar at the American Enterprise Institute when President Ronald Reagan asked her to serve as U.S. Permanent Representative to the United Nations, a post that meant she served in the cabinet and on the National Security Council. Today, she is one of the most renowned women in the nation and one whose name is often mentioned as a potential candidate for vice president and even president of the United States.

The Roots of an Ambassador

Jeane Jordan Kirkpatrick was born November 19, 1926, in Duncan, Oklahoma. At that time Duncan was suffering from both the Great Depression and the drought-induced dust storms that brought about the mass migrations from Oklahoma to other states. Her father, Welcher F. Jordan, was an oil-drilling contractor who sought greater economic opportunities in oil-prosperous south central Illinois. Jeane Kirkpatrick discusses the early influence of her parents by saying that her mother encouraged her to be anything she wanted to be and to study, whereas her father hoped she would marry the boy next door. Neither parent encouraged a career in public service, but she concedes that if they were alive they would have considerable pride in her accomplishments.[2] Her family background and the attitudes of her parents were apparently not very different from those of other middle-class families of that era who valued education and aspired for a better life for their children.

Jeane Jordan was an A student in high school and active in school journalism and drama. She began her higher education at Stephens College in Columbia, Missouri, but graduated from Barnard College in New York City in 1948. She received her M.A. in 1950 and her Ph.D. in 1967, both from Columbia University and both in political science.

In 1955 Jeane Jordan married Evron M. Kirkpatrick, a State Department official who later became executive director of the American Political Science Association. That same year she accepted a position with the Department of Defense and worked intermittently on research for defense contractors until 1972. Early in her career, Kirkpatrick joined her husband in his Democratic party activities. The Kirkpatricks were especially active in Hubert Humphrey's campaigns, and Jeane Kirkpatrick served on several important party committees such as the 1976 National Convention Credentials Committee.

Jeane Kirkpatrick taught part time at Trinity College (1962–1967) and then accepted a position at Georgetown University. In 1978 she became Leavey Professor of Political Science at that institution. Her scholarly contributions to the field of political science include *The New Presidential Elite, Political Woman, Leader and Vanguard in Mass Society,* and articles in the *Journal of Politics* and the *American Political Science Review.* She was a well-established academic when she came to the attention of presidential candidate Ronald Reagan.

The Making of a Conservative

Jeane Kirkpatrick is one of a number of intellectuals who in the late 1960s and early 1970s became disillusioned with the Democratic party, which they believed was moving away from its traditional values. This group, sometimes identified as neoconservative, supported government action to curb social injustice and the welfare state, but they developed serious misgivings about what they considered to be misguided efforts to achieve equal opportunity and liberal policies that they perceived as failing to meet and challenge communist expansionism. At the vanguard of this movement were some of the leaders of the American Political Science Association who were close professional associates of the Kirkpatricks. These leaders did not reflect the political views of the majority of their profession. Political scientists generally tend to identify themselves as "moderately liberal" to "very liberal" and are strongly Democratic.[3] This political stance puts mainstream political scientists squarely at odds with most of the policy positions of Jeane Kirkpatrick and has made her the focus of the criticism and disdain commonly reserved for apostates. The disillusioned Democrats, including Jeane Kirkpatrick, established the Coalition for a Democratic Majority and shared their views through the publications of the American Enterprise Institute and *Commentary* magazine.

In 1979 Richard Allen, Ronald Reagan's principal foreign policy adviser, gave Reagan a copy of "Dictatorships and Double Standards," an article Kirkpatrick had written for *Commentary* that was highly critical of President Jimmy Carter's foreign policy. Reagan arranged for a meeting with Kirkpatrick, and she soon became one of his campaign foreign policy advisers. After the election Reagan asked her to head the U.S. delegation to the United Nations, a post she held longer than any since Adlai E. Stevenson.

Foreign Policy

Dictatorships and Double Standards

Kirkpatrick takes exception to political philosophies based on the premise that absolute equality is an operational social goal. She argues that twentieth century experience indicates that equality is unachievable and that socialist revolutionary regimes seeking to attain it end with a less economically strong society characterized by more limited personal freedom. She does not understand how the myth that the Marxist-Leninist revolution will enhance freedom and improve the quality of life can persist in the face of so much empirical evidence to the contrary. The persistence of the myth, she believes, lies in the rationalism that characterizes so much twentieth-century thought. She writes, "Because it assumes that man and society can be brought to conform to a preferred plan, the rationalist orientation tends powerfully to see everything as possible and prospects for progress as unlimited."[4] She warns, "When we forget or willfully choose to ignore the intractability of human behavior, the complexity of human institutions, and the probability of unanticipated consequences, we do so at great risk, and often immense human cost."[5] This is the thematic base for much of her attack on the Carter foreign policy.

She blames the Carter administration for the loss of the Panama Canal, the decline of U.S. influence in Africa and Latin America, and the failure of the United States to maintain its military power in the light of a strong Soviet military buildup. Her strongest objection, however, is that Carter "actively collaborated in the replacement of moderate autocrats friendly to U.S. interests with less friendly autocrats of extremist persuasion."[6] She is especially concerned about those extremists with strong ties to the communist bloc.

She says the U.S. pattern of response is fairly predictable. An autocratic regime friendly to U.S. interests is attacked by insurgents, who often have communist ties. These communist ties are minimized or ignored by the media and by those U.S. political leaders who contend that our support for the dictator makes it necessary for the insurgents to seek help where it is available. As armed hostility increases, the U.S. public begins to question the ability of the existing government to survive. This questioning is encouraged by reports of human rights violations and appeals to our own revolutionary origins. This is followed by pressures on the administration to take measures to force the regime to liberalize its policies, but these steps are most likely to dilute the regime's power and ultimately its political control. The president's response to the deteriorating situation is to reduce military aid and to seek a political solution. Kirkpatrick argues that it is only after this scenario has been played out and

> anarchy has spread throughout the nation will it be noticed that the new head of government has no significant following, no experience at governing, and no talent for leadership. . . . The United States will have been led by its own misunderstanding of the situation to assist actively in deposing an erstwhile friend and ally and installing a government hostile to American interests and policies of the world. . . . And everywhere our friends will have noted that American support provides no security against the forward march of history.[7]

Although Kirkpatrick acknowledges that this scenario cannot be applied in toto to Iran and Nicaragua, she asserts that it comes close enough to be useful in understanding how crisis situations developed in those countries. Kirkpatrick was especially critical of Carter's contention that his administration would impose sanctions on governments found to violate human rights. She noted that such a stance was impossible to maintain with any consistency and resulted in a double standard that demonstrated the hypocrisy of the administration's foreign policy.

This criticism is consistent with Kirkpatrick's belief that rights are easily claimed but difficult to implement. She says that rationalism deceives us into believing that what can be conceived can be achieved. This self-deception results in an emphasis on motives and neglect of the ethics of consequences.

> Doing what one knows is right becomes more important than producing any given desirable results. In human rights and foreign policy the tendency to prefer an ethic of consequences leads to an overwhelming concern with the purity of the intentions as embodied in our policies. When our motives are viewed as more important than the consequences of our actions, then whatever our policies have in fact contributed to the creation

of a new tyranny in a place like Iran seems to matter less than whether our intentions were good. The principal function of a human rights policy that emphasizes motives rather than consequences is, I believe, to make us feel good about ourselves. It feels good to feel good, to be sure. But one wonders about that as a goal of foreign policy.[8]

Jeane Kirkpatrick's discussions of morality and foreign policy have stimulated considerable debate, as has her interpretation of recent historical events. Her critics equate her position with Franklin D. Roosevelt's comment about Somoza, a former Nicaraguan director: "I know he is a son of a bitch, but he is *our* son of a bitch." Her position is, of course, not universally accepted and is viewed by many as an oversimplification of a very complex issue.

In discussing Kirkpatrick's theories and their manifestation in Reagan's foreign policy, Lincoln Bloomfield of the Massachusetts Institute of Technology says, "We begin to yearn for the branch of conservatism that focuses on realpolitik rather than on the transvaluation of values."[9] Some critics say that she has put herself in a position in which she appears to be defending inhumane acts that are surely repugnant to her. "Kirkpatrick, like many other diplomats before her (and her Soviet counterpart), is selective in what she denounces. Sakharov's exile is bad, but torture in Turkey can be passed over in silence."[10]

Her assertation that the ultimate goal is to achieve democracy also is challenged. "An administration which seeks pleasant relations with every right-wing thug in the hemisphere is simply unconvincing when it claims to be struggling for democracy in Central America."[11] There is fear that Kirkpatrick's denial of moral equivalency, especially between Soviet and U.S. behavior, can lead to justification for any and all U.S. action. In expressing this concern, Alex Nove writes:

> The USSR is not Nazi Germany, and we are not at war. It does bother me if our side, in understandable anxiety not to lose the peace, uses morally repugnant methods treating any anticommunist thug as an honorary member of the "free world." It bothers me not just because I have a few scruples, but because this way one unnecessarily makes enemies and causes divisions among friends. A little self-criticism would not come amiss.[12]

Joseph Nye joins the discussion by criticizing what he believes to be Kirkpatrick's overemphasis on moral consequences. He reminds us of the pitfalls of what he describes as "one-dimensional ethics." Although actions can be justified in terms of motives or consequences, in practice we make ethical judgments on the basis of motives, means, and consequences, and this forces us to balance competing moral claims. "Ends, means, and consequences are all important."[13]

The Policy in Practice

There is little doubt that Jeane Kirkpatrick has had a substantial impact on the Reagan administration's foreign policy. During her tenure as U.S. ambassador she had easy and direct access to the president, often to the chagrin of two secretaries of state, Alexander Haig and George Schultz.[14] Reagan's acceptance of Kirkpatrick's theses was more noticeable during his first term in office. Reagan's handling of the Philippine crisis in early 1986 may represent a move away from Kirkpatrick's position and an acceptance of the inevitability of Marcos' departure.

After her resignation as U.N. ambassador, she continued to promote her foreign policy views in her speeches and newspaper columns. Kirkpatrick saw criticism of Marcos as one more example of the scenario discussed earlier that had plagued and threatened U.S. national interest. She believed that the Philippines' strategic position made it critical for us to have a friendly government in power, and she lamented the press's treatment of "Marcos' real and imagined failures, inefficiencies and corruption as though they were extraordinary and unique." She pointed out, "Of 159 member states of the United Nations, at least 100 are probably governed more poorly than the Philippines."[15] She warned that the fall of Marcos could lead to a more repressive government as similar events had in Cuba, Vietnam, Iran, and Nicaragua.

Kirkpatrick's warnings and advice regarding the Philippines did not prevail. Reagan's policy toward the end of the Marcos and Duvalier regimes was surprisingly similar to Carter's approach of publicly chiding recalcitrant leaders and finally helping to force them out of office when other pressures were ineffective. It appears, especially in the Philippines, that the new leadership will more closely resemble the more democratic leaders that replaced dictatorships in Spain, Portugal, Argentina, Brazil, and Guatemala than the despots predicted by Kirkpatrick.[16] It is undoubtedly true that a strong democratic tradition and the existence of a strong middle class in the Philippines facilitated the political transition, but it also suggests that the United States would do well to encourage a moderate opposition before extremists gain acceptance as the only viable alternative.[17]

The United Nations

Jeane Kirkpatrick has described her first nine months in the United Nations as one of the most intensive learning experiences of her life.[18] She found herself in an institution rigid with conventions, rituals, and deep-rooted practices—and with sanctions for those who strayed from accepted behavior. As was the case with earlier U.S. ambassadors, Kirkpatrick often found herself defending a minority position. She discovered it was the practice to ignore attacks on the United States on the grounds that it was demeaning for a powerful nation to respond to weaker states. She refused to accept this custom and responded to any and all significant attacks. She sent copies of anti-U.S. speeches to U.S. embassies in the appropriate countries so that governments would become more aware of and sensitive to the actions of their delegates. She sent the voting records of all member nations to Congress. She threatened to cut aid from nations that consistently opposed our positions on the premise that we were weakening our stance in the United Nations by refusing to discriminate between supporters and opponents. She concluded that we had been relatively ineffective in the United Nations because we had not acquired the necessary skills to function successfully in a multinational arena.[19] "By not really learning the rules, the players, the game, we have often behaved like a bunch of amateurs in the United Nations. Unless or until we approach the United Nations as professionals . . . with a clear-cut conception of our purposes, and of the political arena in which we operate . . . we won't ever know whether the United Nations could be made a hospitable place for the American national interest."[20]

Her strong position was often effective, and she is credited with the defeat of resolutions to expel Israel from the United Nations, the defeat of Cuba's efforts to chastise the United States for "colonizing" Puerto Rico, and the defeat of Nicaragua's efforts to condemn U.S. policy in Central America.[21] Some U.N. observers believed that she could have achieved the same goals with less moralizing and with more patient and diplomatic tactics, but it is also likely that her style would have been less objectionable in a male.

Jeane Kirkpatrick's service as ambassador was made more difficult by Secretary of State Alexander Haig's lack of support and his efforts to undermine her influence and achievements. For example, when Kirkpatrick succeeded in negotiating a unanimous resolution that condemned Israel for bombing Iraq's nuclear reactors, but stopped short of sanctions, some State Department officials told reporters that Kirkpatrick had originally supported more extreme measures against Israel, but Haig had been able to intervene and negotiate directly with the Iraqis. The purpose of this misleading assertion was apparently to detract from Kirkpatrick's political coup.[22]

Kirkpatrick was often the victim of leaks to the media that were incomplete, sometimes inaccurate, and appeared to originate from the State Department or the White House staff. She found the experience both distasteful and depressing. In an interview in the *Washington Post* she described the frustrations of working in a hostile environment: "I don't think I bear up very well under it. Intrinsically, I am not very combative—despite my large reputation to the contrary. I have no zest for conflict."[23]

Kirkpatrick especially resents being characterized as a right-wing extremist and anti-Democrat, especially on Central America. "Actually, inside administration policy discussions, I probably have opposed the use of force by the United States in Central America more often and more strongly than any member of this government. I don't mean the use of U.S. combat troops, because nobody's suggested that. I mean any kind of force, even in principle."[24] She continues, "I have the recurring thought, which is what Harry Truman said: 'If you can't stand the heat, get out of the kitchen.' My version of that is: If you can't stand the heat, go back to the kitchen—where I have been very happy. I like private life."[25]

Kirkpatrick the Woman

When the Kirkpatricks' first son, Douglas, was born in 1956, Jeane Kirkpatrick became a full-time homemaker and did not return to work until her third son started the first grade. The break between her master's degree in 1950 and her Ph.D. in 1967 is not uncommon among women with family and childrearing responsibilities. She did not view this as a period of confinement but rather as a time to enjoy the nurturing of her children while continuing to develop her own intellectual interests.[26] "I think any woman who voluntarily deals herself out of motherhood is making a terrible mistake. Similarly, though, if a woman declines to develop her intellectual, aesthetic or professional skills, she also is dealing herself out of major life experiences. Why should anybody voluntarily truncate her life in such a fashion? My motto is 'refuse to choose.'"[27]

Jeane Kirkpatrick's earliest significant contribution to the field of political science was her book *Political Woman*. In 1974, when that book was published, there was a minimal interest among political scientists in the subject of women and politics, and few scholars were interested in researching the subject. Kirkpatrick's study of women legislators, their recruitment into politics, and their political styles was a seminal work that helped legitimize the academic study of women.[28]

When Jeane Kirkpatrick chose a career in political science, she entered a profession dominated by men. As late as 1981 only 11 percent of all political science full-time positions in universities were held by women.[29] In 1969 a group of female political scientists founded the Women's Caucus for Political Science in an effort to improve the status of women within the profession. Kirkpatrick was not one of its original members, but this is not surprising in light of her husband's position as executive director of the American Political Science Association. Kirkpatrick's hesitation in joining was reinforced by her perception that the Women's Caucus was tied to the Caucus for a New Political Science. This latter group contended that political activity and scholarship were inseparable and campaigned to have the American Political Science Association officially take a stand against the Vietnam War and racial discrimination and in support of Lyndon Johnson's War on Poverty programs.[30] In 1972, when Kirkpatrick was convinced that the Women's Caucus was not aligned with the New Caucus and that it was fully committed to improving and promoting the professional status of women in political science, she joined the organization. Although she was never active in the group, she lent her support and still maintains the friendship and respect of the women who worked with her during her membership.

Sexism and Political Life

Kirkpatrick acknowledges that some of the difficulties she experienced at the United Nations were gender-based. Early in her appointment she encountered what she termed "the process of disqualification."[31] U.N. culture is unusually title conscious; she was never called Doctor or Professor but Mrs. Instead of being described as "professorial," she was "schoolmarmish." When she took strong positions in support of United States policy, she was "confrontational." Kirkpatrick is convinced that women in positions of power will inevitably be described as "tough" and "confrontational" because society is not prepared to accept them in this new role.[32] This negative response is not limited to the international arena. In discussing her problems with leaks to reporters, Kirkpatrick speculated that the leaks may have occurred partially because some individuals resented women in high political office.[33]

It is worth observing that many political conservatives who are not noted for their support of women have come to Kirkpatrick's defense. The *National Review* lamented the attacks on Jeane Kirkpatrick and editorialized that

> she is said to be difficult to work with. It is said of her that she is erratic and the word most frequently used is that she is "temperamental." If, by the way, you are in the market for examples of male chauvinism, watch when they use the word "temperamental." They are usually talking about Arturo Toscanini, or a woman. The word has been used so frequently about Jeane Kirkpatrick that John Lofton . . . asked in his column, "Is it intended to suggest that Mrs. Kirkpatrick is temperamental once a month?"[34]

Since she left her United Nations post and started lecturing and writing, she has noted considerable interest in her income. As she does not observe the same interest in Henry Kissinger's fees, she concludes that sexism is once again involved.[35] Jeane Kirkpatrick is disturbed by sexism but will not permit it to make her angry. She counsels women, "If you can avoid the pitfalls of rage and paranoia and can hang in long enough to prove your seriousness and competence . . . then you can develop good relations based on mutual respect with almost all your colleagues."[36]

Feminist Issues

Kirkpatrick is acutely aware of the realities of being a woman in U.S. society. She has proved to be an intelligent and articulate woman who can hold her own among any of our current political leaders. In her professional life she has been supportive of women and by her own example has made it possible for women to move into areas formerly restricted to men. Her personal philosophy on this issue is summarized in her *Who's Who in America* biographical listing.

> My experience demonstrates to my satisfaction that it is both possible and feasible for women in our times to successfully combine traditional and professional roles, that it is not necessary to ape men's career patterns,— starting early and keeping one's nose to a particular grindstone, but that, instead, one can do quite different things at different stages of one's life. All that is required is a little luck and a lot of work.[37]

Her position on feminist issues distinguishes her from many of her conservative colleagues, although these issues do not appear to be high on her political agenda. She supports the Equal Rights Amendment but has not actively campaigned on its behalf. Her position on abortion has been described as "mixed," which aligns her with the majority of U.S. public opinion. When questioned about abortion, she replied, "Basically, I believe abortion is always tragic, always to be avoided. But it is not invariably the worst possible evil in every situation."[38] That very honest response is not likely to satisfy anyone on either of the two extreme sides of the issue.

In August 1984 at the Republican National Convention, Kirkpatrick identified herself as a "welfare state liberal." More recently she described herself as a "welfare state conservative" who still supports day care, Head Start, and child health programs.[39] When asked about Ronald Reagan's policies and their impact on women, Kirkpatrick responded that the feminization of poverty is largely the result of increasing divorce, desertion, and the single parent household, and Reagan could not be held responsible for these.[40] However, she still supports the proposition that government has a responsibility to provide for those unable to care for themselves and criticizes Republicans who are more concerned with financial problems than with human values.[41]

The Political Future

Since Jeane Kirkpatrick joined the Republican party in April 1985, she has been hailed as a potential candidate for national office. In a nationwide telephone survey of contributors to conservative organizations, Kirkpatrick ranked behind Vice President George Bush and senators Robert Dole and Jesse Helm but ahead of such Republican leaders as Howard Baker, Jack

Kemp, and Paul Laxalt as first choice to succeed Reagan.[42] She is often mentioned as a logical vice presidential choice for a male candidate interested in balancing a ticket. Whether this popularity will withstand the pressures of time is a matter for conjecture.

Kirkpatrick has been a student of politics and a political activist long enough to appreciate the benefits and the costs of seeking public office. She was enthusiastic when Walter Mondale chose Geraldine Ferraro as his vice presidential running mate, for Kirkpatrick recognized the significance of that event for the future role of women in U.S. politics. In the midst of the 1984 political campaign, when Ferraro came under attack because of her husband's business dealings and her initial unwillingness to make full financial disclosure, Kirkpatrick reflected on the implications of Ferraro's problem for women considering national office. In an interview with the editors of *Time* magazine, Kirkpatrick commented, "I think the price for participation in high-level politics in our society is very, very high—for both men and women. . . . It is a very harsh game, and I do not think women want whatever it is at the end of that particular rainbow badly enough to pursue it. There are already more opportunities for women in politics than there are women ready to pay the price."[43]

Is Jeane Kirkpatrick willing to pay the price?

If she decides to run for office, Jeane Kirkpatrick would undoubtedly appeal to some women who admire her feminist positions, but her running will create a predicament for feminists who have serious concerns about her position on foreign policy. Donna E. Shalala, president of Hunter College and a liberal Democrat, summarizes this dilemma well. She says, "Jeane is extraordinarily complex. She has a strong commitment to women's issues, a real sensitivity and I like her. It would be very tough for me to vote for her, because of her international views. But I'd think about it—I wouldn't just knee-jerk, 'No.'"[44]

Undoubtedly Jeane Kirkpatrick would make an interesting candidate and bring a new dimension to U.S. campaign politics. Robert Goodman, a Republican media consultant, predicts that if Kirkpatrick decides to run, it will be a campaign with a new twist. "She'll make serious speeches and she'll take strong positions on controversial issues, and people will regard her not so much as a candidate with political ambitions but more as an American leader with convictions."[45] For Jeane Kirkpatrick that will not be a new role.

Notes

1. Jane Rosen, "The Kirkpatrick Factor," *New York Times Magazine,* April 28, 1985, 48.

2. James R. Whelan, "Jeane Kirkpatrick: Ideals Come First," *Saturday Evening*

Post (December 1984):42. Also see Anne Tremblay, "Jeane Kirkpatrick," *Working Woman* (May 1983):108.

3. Naomi B. Lynne, "Self-Portrait: Profile of Political Scientists," in Ada W. Finifter, ed., *Political Science: The State of the Discipline* (Washington, D.C.: American Political Science Association, 1983), 110, 111.

4. Jeane J. Kirkpatrick, *Dictatorships and Double Standards: Rationalism and Reason in Politics* (New York: The American Enterprise Institute and Simon and Schuster, 1982), 17, 18.

5. Ibid., 18.

6. Ibid., 23.

7. Ibid., 26–28.

8. Jeane J. Kirkpatrick, *The Reagan Phenomenon: And Other Speeches on Foreign Policy* (Washington, D.C.: The American Institute for Public Policy Research, 1983), 43.

9. Lincoln P. Bloomfield, "Transvalued Values and Common Sense," *Society* 22 (March-April 1985):11.

10. Alec Nove, "The Scope and Scale of Good and Evil," *Society* 22 (March-April 1985):13, 14.

11. Ibid., 13.

12. Ibid., 16.

13. Joseph S. Nye, Jr., "Motives, Means and Consequences," *Society* 22 (March-April 1985):17–20.

14. Rosen, "The Kirkpatrick Factor," 51.

15. Jeane J. Kirkpatrick, "Marcos and the Purists," *Washington Post,* December 16, 1985, A-15.

16. Mark Whitaker, John Walcott, and Peter McKillop, "How To Deal with Dictators," *Newsweek,* March 10, 1986, 35–37.

17. Ibid.

18. Kirkpatrick, *The Reagan Phenomenon,* 79.

19. Ibid., 103–104.

20. Ibid., 105.

21. Rosen, "The Kirkpatrick Factor," 69.

22. Tremblay, "Jeane Kirkpatrick," 109.

23. Lally Weymouth, "Why Tolerate Sniping White House Aides, Leaks and Unfair Labels?" *Washington Post,* December 2, 1984, D-3.

24. Ibid.

25. Ibid., D-4.

26. Whelan, "Jeane Kirkpatrick: Ideals Come First," 54.

27. Tremblay, "Jeane Kirkpatrick," 108.

28. Jeane J. Kirkpatrick, *Political Woman* (New York: Basic Books, 1974).

29. Lynn, "Self Portrait," 118.

30. Ibid., 115.

31. Jeane J. Kirkpatrick, "Why I Think More Women Are Needed at the Pinnacle of World Politics," *Glamour* 83 (September 1985):178.

32. Ibid., 178.

33. Ibid.

34. "Exit Jeane Kirkpatrick," *National Review,* December 28, 1984, 54.

35. Fred Barnes, "Queen Jeane," *The New Republic,* July 8, 1985, 10.

36. Kirkpatrick, "Why I Think More Women Are Needed," 180.

37. *Who's Who in America,* vol. 1 (Chicago: Marquis Who's Who, 1982–1983), 1823.

38. William Rasberry, "Kirkpatrick on Abortion," *Washington Post,* July 29, 1985, A-13.

39. Barnes, "Queen Jeane," 9, 10.

40. Betty Cuniberti, "Kirkpatrick Sidesteps Role in 'Gender Gap,'" *Los Angeles Times,* August 20, 1984, I:4.

41. Rosen, "The Kirkpatrick Factor," 71.

42. Andrew Mollison, "Kirkpatrick Scores Well in GOP Poll," *Atlanta Journal and Constitution,* February 2, 1986, 14.

43. Jeane Kirkpatrick, "Making the Price Too High," *Time,* September 3, 1984, 18.

44. Rosen, "The Kirkpatrick Factor," 71.

45. Ibid.

Barbara Mikulski: Representing the Neighborhood

JANE P. SWEENEY

"If I bring recognition to myself, I'll bring recognition to my community, to Baltimore. I feel very emotional about the pride this brings to the people in my neighborhood."[1] This was Barbara Mikulski's reaction to a journalist's question about how she felt after being asked by Senator Edward Kennedy to nominate him for the presidency at the 1980 Democratic Convention. It is also a comment that reveals a core characteristic of Barbara Mikulski: a deep love for and commitment to her neighborhood roots. She began her political career because she wanted to get on the inside of the power structure to fight for her people.

After serving on the Baltimore City Council from 1971 to 1976, Barbara Mikulski was elected to Congress in 1976 and successfully reelected to four additional terms in the House. In November 1986 she was elected to the Senate by a large margin and is now the only Democratic woman in that body. This chapter examines her political career and the forces that shaped her liberal politics. Several themes prevail: the neighborhood, a commitment to feminism, a belief in the need for the powerless to organize.

The Development of a Political Philosophy

Barbara Mikulski was born on July 20, 1936, in the same East Baltimore neighborhood where she lives today. She is the granddaughter of Polish immigrants and is fiercely proud of her heritage. Her father owned a small grocery store and Mikulski asserts that as a result, "the neighborhood was really our extended family. . . . If Bethlehem Steel was on strike, my father extended credit to the guys. In the middle of a snowstorm, if he didn't see Miss Sophie, who was a diabetic, he called down there to see if she needed anything. I ran down the oranges."[2]

105

In another description of her youth, the Mikulski sense of humor reveals itself. She was introducing Senator Kennedy at a fund-raising dinner. After noting the similarities in their backgrounds—ethnic roots, close families—she added, "Our fathers were both entrepreneurs. My father owned a small grocery store. Your father owned Boston."[3]

Mikulski was educated in Catholic schools for sixteen years, graduating in 1958 from Mount St. Agnes College. Seven years later she received her M.S.W. from the University of Maryland School of Social Work. She was employed as a social worker by Catholic Charities and by the Baltimore Welfare Department.

Mikulski is a liberal who was influenced in the late 1960s by three individuals: Saul Alinsky, Monsignor Geno Baroni, and Dorothy Day.[4] Alinsky, the Chicago-based activist and author of *Reville for Radicals,* provided the theory on which her first successful community organizing projects were based. "Power never yields voluntarily. . . . Power is not only what you have, but what the enemy thinks you have." Baroni was director of the National Center for Urban Ethnic Affairs and later an undersecretary at the Department of Housing and Urban Development during the Carter administration. When Baroni and Mikulski first met in 1970 they discussed the critical importance of building coalitions among ethnic minorities in a political world that sought to play "divide and conquer" with ethnic groups. Day was the founder of Catholic Worker, an organization based in New York City which fed and sheltered the homeless and encouraged a sense of close community among its members. The philosophy of Catholic Worker was that belief in Christianity would result in positive social action on behalf of the poor. Mikulski's political career shows that the same values motivate her.

An interesting facet of Mikulski's career is that although she is often associated, because of the causes in which she believes, with the "limousine liberals" of the Democratic party's left wing, she retains a deep loyalty to the ethnic community and its institutions, particularly the Catholic church. In 1970, when the *New York Times* described her as a "young Polish American and a member of a Baltimore community organization," she wrote a guest column called "Who Speaks for Urban America?" In this article (as throughout her career), she maintained that the country's working-class ethnic populations "made a maximum contribution to the USA, yet received minimal recognition."[5] She was concerned that working-class families were losing ground economically and that government policies were polarizing the black and white working class. She was bothered that liberals scapegoated the white ethnics as racists. "The elitists who now smugly call us racists are the ones who taught us the meaning of the word: their bigotry extended to those of a different class or national origin." She wanted to be sure that the old neighborhoods would not be demolished in the name of urban renewal.

The one place where he [the ethnic] felt the master of his fate and had status was in his own neighborhood. Now even that security is being threatened. He wants new schools for his children and recreation facilities for the entire family. . . . He wants the streets fixed and the garbage collected. He finds that the only things being planned for his area are housing projects, expressways and fertilizer factories. When he goes to City Hall to make his problems known, he is either put off, put down or put out.

In 1970 Mikulski, the Geno Baroni disciple, argued that ethnic and racial minorities needed to develop alliances through community organizing. A few years later she was still writing about the larger society's lack of sensitivity to its ethnic populations. This time she turned her attention to the problems and discomfort of working-class women in particular. She wrote about women who told her of "their deep pain at perceiving their ethnicity viewed as quaint and cute; their neighborhoods as being on the other side of the tracks; their life styles as unhip and their values as unsophisticated."[6] Although herself a woman who broke the mold of what was expected of women in her community, she retained a great understanding of what was happening to working-class women in Baltimore. She was aware that the value changes of the 1960s were almost too much for working-class families to endure, that the need for many women without skills to return to the work force was a terrible strain, that our models no longer served the young generation. In fact, one can argue that her feminism is largely informed by her empathy for working-class women and her respect for the contributions to U.S. society made by Catholic sisters.

Although Mikulski can be critical of what she views as patriarchal attitudes and sexism within the church, her respect for the contemporary Catholic sisterhood is huge. She clearly acknowledges the important role of the church schools staffed by sisters in the ethnic communities.

> I think that among many Catholics, particularly many of us of a very liberal persuasion, that it was often fashionable to trivialize, minimize or even ridicule the great parochial school system out of which so many of us came. . . . I remember that for my mother and the other great families of immigrants before us, the parochial school system was the bridge between the old world and the new. . . . For those of us they called Dagos and Wops and Hunkies and so on, we were the ones who came to this country to try to make it great. However, they wanted our bodies for work but we found they didn't want us to participate in the society they had established. Yet in that parochial school . . . what we found was a home.[7]

Not only does Mikulski salute the social services provided by the Catholic sisters in the past, she encourages Catholic sisters today to "reclaim Christianity from the Right Wing." She argues that "Jerry Falwell and his crowd are giving God a bad name. They're using new time religion to peddle old time prejudice. . . . I'm upset about how we take the traditional values of mother-hood and twist them and somehow or another imply that if the Blessed Mother were around today, she'd be against the ERA."[8] Mikulski is close to a Washington-based lobby called Network, an organization of Catholic sisters that espouses liberal political causes, supports women's organizations, and argues for female ordination to the priesthood.

In Mikulski we find a woman who wants to preserve the old neighbor-hoods, and who is a feminist, an organizer, a bridge builder. The impulse to political organizing came in the late 1960s when Mikulski discovered that a sixteen-lane interstate highway was about to be built through the heart of *her* neighborhood.[9] At the time her career as a social worker was leading her to conclude that the very structure of power in society caused many of its problems, and she was disturbed about growing tension between Poles and blacks in her neighborhood. Angered about the highway and aware that organizing the community was a means to alleviate polarization, she founded SCAR (Southeast Committee Against the Road). Later SCAR merged with an adjoining middle-class neighborhood to form SECO (Southeast Community Organization). SECO brought in a professional organizer who was a disciple of Alinsky, the road was not built, the group became one of the most successful community organizations in the United States, and Mikulski loved every minute of it.

SECO started small, but as soon as progress on the interstate highway issue had been achieved, it expanded and took on other local problems. Meanwhile, Mikulski began to realize that her tactics in Baltimore might have to diverge from Alinsky's in Chicago. Alinsky knew that in Chicago elec-toral politics were under the total control of the Daly machine, so he had to fight from the outside. Mikulski began to think that the best way to operate in Baltimore was to seek electoral office. "As we worked on all these is-sues . . . I became convinced that the answer was in politics. Every door we went to was a political door. . . . All roads led to either City Hall or the Statehouse or Washington. And rather than being on the other side banging on the door, I wanted to be where the action was."[10]

A Political Career

In 1971 Barbara Mikulski ran for the Baltimore City Council and won. She spent five years on the City Council before running successfully for the House of Representatives in 1976. Even before she took national office, how-ever, she began to exercise her influence on the state and national levels. In 1972, after the Democratic party leadership decided that the quota system used at that year's national convention had been disastrous for the party, Mikulski was appointed to a commission to rewrite the delegate selection rules. One year later the commission's chair, Leonard Woodcock of the United Auto Workers, resigned, and Mikulski became chairwoman. Although this was not a position of great public prominence, it gave Mikulski the opportunity to become known among the national elite of her party.

In 1974 Barbara Mikulski made an unsuccessful bid for the Senate seat of Charles Mathias, a liberal Republican. She managed to win the Democratic nomination owing to her strong support in Baltimore but did not have the funding for an adequate statewide campaign for the general election. Still, she managed to win 43 percent of the statewide vote. Charles Mathias retired in 1986, and in liberal Maryland Mikulski won an easy victory over conservative Republican Linda Chavez.

In 1976 Mikulski won 75 percent of the vote in her heavily Democratic district and entered the House. Maryland's Third Congressional District is dominated by the blue-collar neighborhoods in which Mikulski was raised. The area is replete with ethnic communities and is populated by people who work in heavy industry. In 1980 the Third Congressional District was redistricted, and Mikulski became representative of several suburban neighborhoods, but even these areas tend to have liberal voting records. Within Baltimore she represents Otterbein, a neighborhood where young professionals have restored old brownstones. In the suburbs her district includes the planned community of Columbia. The town was designed as an idealistic socioeconomic experiment including, for example, subsidized housing units scattered around the community. About 20 percent of the population is black, and the citizens on the whole are quite liberal.

Election results in the Third District seem to indicate that Mikulski had a safe seat in the House for as long as she wanted it. After her 1976 victory, she ran uncontested in the 1978 general election. In 1980 and 1982 she won 76 percent and 74 percent of the vote respectively. In 1984, when two people ran against her in the Democratic primary, she still won 89 percent of that vote, a virtual reassurance of reelection in her district. In fact, in 1976 and 1980 she won very solid majorities while the national ticket just squeaked through in the district. In 1984 she won handily while Ronald Reagan carried the presidential race in her district.

Various indices of Mikulski's voting record place her firmly in the liberal camp. In terms of support for the president, Mikulski's ratings changed dramatically with the election of Ronald Reagan. Under Carter her votes in support of the president ranged from 70 to 78 percent during four years. Under Reagan they dropped to 31 percent in 1981 and have stayed in that range. In fact, she is one of Congress' most outspoken critics of Reagan policies. In 1981 she said of the first Reagan budget:

> What we did was wage war against women and children and old people and underdogs. And what we said is "We have money for bankers, but we

don't have money for shelters for battered women. We have money for nerve gas, but we don't have money for health care. We have money for the MX missile, but we don't have money to run schools and buy hearing aids and braces for crippled children."[11]

Mikulski, a reform-minded Democrat, has a strong record of voting with her party. Between the years 1977 and 1982 her voting record in terms of party unity ranged from a low of 84 percent in 1981 to a high of 92 percent in 1980. In fact, although some expected that she would act in the House in a rather cantankerous style, she has often made cool, pragmatic choices. An example of this style was her first vote for House Majority leader. Liberals were surprised when she supported conservative Jim Wright of Texas, but Wright won, and Mikulski's vote resulted in excellent committee assignments for a first-time congresswoman.

Interest group ratings also demonstrate a consistently liberal voting pattern. Mikulski's annual ratings from the Americans for Democratic Action (ADA) have ranged from 84 percent in 1979 to 100 percent in 1981. Likewise, the AFL-CIO has rated her support for organized labor from a low of 83 percent in 1980 to 100 percent in 1982. As might be expected, the Americans for Conservative Action has rated her as low as 7 percent and never higher than 27 percent.

Ten years in the House of Representatives has provided substantial evidence about the types of issues Mikulski supports. Referring to herself as a "commonsense" democrat, she comments about economic issues.

I want a strong economy. I believe we must make a downpayment on our deficit. We must make trade a two way street. We must meet our social responsibility and keep our fiscal responsibility. I believe that people who work hard for their money should get to keep it. And I believe that tax breaks should not only go to the people who can afford high-paid tax experts.[12]

This passage is the essential Mikulski. She is concerned about jobs in her port city, about necessary social programs, about fairness in the tax structure. Therefore, she is an outspoken critic of giving the Pentagon every cent it wants and has voted for some cuts in the defense budget. She also is strongly opposed to the Gramm-Rudman solution to our budgetary problems.

The Mikulski view on national security is a distinct contrast to that of Ronald Reagan. As she sees it, we are wrong to use the size of the defense budget as a measure of how secure we are. Of all defense spending, the current escalation of the nuclear arms race is of greatest concern to her. She believes that our poor record on human rights abroad under the Reagan administration adversely affects our reputation and hence our long-term security.

Education has been one of Mikulski's major concerns throughout her career, and at present she is very concerned about the effects of Reagan budgets on the country's future. Writing in 1985 she pointed out that under four years of Ronald Reagan, federal funding for education fell by 21.5 percent. "In real terms that means we have seen 900,000 disadvantaged children lose their education benefits; we have seen education for handicapped children fall 9.1%; and we have witnessed a 30% drop in federal vocational education programs."[13] She believes the federal role in education should be strengthened, while the pragmatist in her thinks one possible federal role is to encourage business to donate expensive technological equipment to schools. She has introduced legislation to that effect.

The nature of her district and her own working-class background should make it obvious that Mikulski is active in promoting growth in job opportunities. Here, she thinks economic growth is the only long-term solution and advocates policies to stabilize international currency values so U.S. firms can compete abroad. In the interim she supports job training programs for minority teenagers, displaced homemakers, and workers over fifty in danger of losing their jobs to new technologies.

Mikulski has been active in efforts to enforce hazardous waste laws and to clean up the environment, and much of her committee work has focused on these concerns. She is also an advocate of increased federal funding for health care, protection from occupational diseases, and consumer information regarding health care. This pragmatist introduced "good guy" legislation that rewards states that reduce hospital costs. If a state can demonstrate greater cost efficiency in its hospital system, federal Medicaid cuts it might have suffered are not made. In 1981 alone this added $9 million to Maryland's Medicaid funds.

Mikulski's record on a few major votes demonstrates how she carries out her philosophy on the floor of the House. In foreign policy, she supported the Panama Canal treaties in 1979. In 1980 she voted to aid the Sandinista regime in Nicaragua, and in 1986 she opposed President Reagan's request for $100 million in aid to the Nicaraguan contras. These votes are consistent with her concern about strengthening our national security by improving our image abroad. It also should be noted that Mikulski has been increasingly interested in foreign policy, particularly in Central America. The catalyst for this interest was the murder of four U.S. churchwomen in El Salvador in 1981. On defense-related issues, she has opposed funding the MX missile and has approved the congressional resolution advocating a nuclear freeze.

On domestic issues we find the same consistency between her philosophy and her voting record. She voted, for example, to guarantee loans to the Chrysler Corporation in 1979, a vote clearly connected with her concern about jobs. We also find her voting to strengthen fair housing laws and to reauthorize the Legal Services Administration. She routinely votes against Reagan's budget proposals. She also voted against the 1982 proposal for the balanced budget constitutional amendment and the 1986 Gramm-Rudman bill.

Committee assignments can make or break a congressional career because it is so important that a Representative be able to work in favor of the concerns of her/his district. One of the classic stories about a committee assignment designed to bury a new member of the House involves Shirley Chisholm of Brooklyn. Representing an absolutely urban constituency, Chisholm was assigned to the Agriculture Committee because the party leadership was displeased with her. Chisholm fought her way to better committee assignments and perhaps the House leadership began to learn that women members would not be pushed around. Mikulski fared much better on her initial committee assignments. She did not get Ways and Means, which was her first choice, but her assignments allowed her to do two crucial things: to serve the needs of Baltimore and to advance issues that interest her, such as women's rights, worker safety, consumer rights, and clean air. Assignment to the Merchant Marine and Fisheries Committee might not seem particularly interesting to a consumerist and feminist, but that committee has important jurisdiction of the port of Baltimore so it provides Mikulski with the opportunity to serve her constituents. She chairs Merchant Marine's Oceanography Subcommittee and also sits on the Coast Guard and Merchant Marine subcommittees.

Mikulski's other committee is Energy and Commerce, and as a member of this committee she is able to exercise influence on a number of issues of great interest to her. She sits on two subcommittees, Health and the Environment and Commerce, Transportation, and Tourism. The Energy and Commerce Committee's scope is quite broad; in this context Mikulski almost always votes with the environmentalist faction. Here she worked hard for strong "superfund" legislation requiring chemical companies to pay for cleanup of toxic wastes and for the Environmental Protection Agency to enforce tough standards.

The problems posed for environmentalists, however, are well illustrated by the problem of trying to pass a stringent Clean Air Act in 1982. In the Health Subcommittee Mikulski and the environmentalists consistently lost votes on amendment after amendment designed to strengthen the bill. Mikulski voted against the proposed bill, but then voted nevertheless to send it to full committee. The *Washington Post* accused Mikulski of giving in to industry pressure because of a General Motors plant in her district. Mikulski was quick to write to the *Post* and make clear that she voted to send on a bill with which she was unhappy because it was the only bill.[14] On the whole, it is frustrating for Mikulski and allies like Jim Florio (D-NJ) to get tough environmental legislation out of the committee, but their failures are not for lack of effort.

In 1984 Mikulski, Florio, and Commerce Committee chair John Dingell (D-Mich) sponsored legislation to end discrimination in insurance rates. The bill was to be Title III of the Economic Equity Act and was supported by a broad coalition of women's and civil rights groups. In a mark-up session described as "contentious," opponents of the bill managed to strike out its major reforms, and the three co-sponsors withdrew their bill.[15] Mikulski was particularly angered by amendments regarding insurance plans that provided either maternity or insurance coverage. "One amendment penalizes us for having children, and one amendment penalizes us for not having them."[16]

The most skillful legislator does not win every battle, but Barbara Mikulski has won a good many. She can point to important victories on consumer and safety issues, and she has served Baltimore well. Her ten years in the House certainly proved she had the qualifications to advance to the Senate.

Mikulski the Feminist

Barbara Mikulski, when discussing the treatment—or lack thereof—of women in U.S. history books, remarked that

> American women throughout our history have been leaders of revolution and social change, but you certainly wouldn't know it from the history books. Any foreigner or visitor from a third or fourth planet looking at pictures of our founding fathers would never know there had been founding mothers. . . . If you look at the book again, there were Pilgrim women, they always showed Pilgrim women! I feel that one of the reasons they showed Pilgrim women so prominently is that they had to demonstrate that someone had to serve those turkeys![17]

When Mikulski arrived in Congress news of her strong feminist convictions preceded her. It was expected by many that she would be "confrontational" in the style of Bella Abzug (a style I must admit to enjoying), and in an institution that is still largely an old boys club, contentious women are not well liked. Mikulski has skillfully used her marvelous sense of humor and innate political savvy to advantage in breaking down stereotypes and forging alliances. This should come as no surprise from a woman who has the strong allegiance of the working-class men in her district. She is very active in the Congressional Caucus on Women's Issues, but she has not neglected other areas. She knows that toxic waste, unemployment, and nuclear disarmament affect women every bit as much as they affect men.

Mikulski did not begin her political career to advance narrowly defined women's issues, but rather to stop a road from decimating her neighborhood. Yet, as is the case for many women discussed in this volume, participation in the political process has led her to become very closely associated with the promotion of feminist causes. She is an outspoken advocate of the Equal Rights Amendment and supported the extension of the ratification deadline. She is also willing to get into nitty-gritty issues like pay equity, retraining of displaced homemakers, and equality of treatment by insurance companies. Her committee assignments allow her to pursue legislative action on these concerns. On the subject of an amendment to ban legal abortion, she spoke with characteristic bluntness to an audience of Catholic sisters.

> In this country today, we now say that women should not be included in the Constitution of the United States, that it is not *needed* to include women in the Constitution of the United States! . . . While they keep us out of the Constitution, so we can't demand full protection under the law, they want us in the Constitution in a different way to be able to control our wombs. Is that what this country should be like? No, I don't think so.[18]

Mikulski makes an argument offered by others who take a pro-choice position—that it is the Reagan administration and not they who are antifamily. "The President says he is for the right-to-life and I believe that. But at the same time, what he did to his health care budget with its proposed cuts in the nutrition program that would have assisted pregnant women belies that statement. At the same time he eliminated child welfare and adoption services so people would have no other alternative."[19]

Mikulski is not doctrinaire, but she is deeply committed to forging an equal place for women in the laws and economic system of the United States. Whatever her political future, one can expect her to continue espousing a liberal feminist position on issues affecting women and to do so with a joke when that helps the cause.

The Future

Many prominent Congresswomen have been unable to make the jump from the House to the Senate, but Mikulski did so on November 4, 1986. In a state where registered Democratic voters outnumber Republicans by four to one, and with her strong base in Baltimore County, Barbara Mikulski won 61 percent of the votes cast. It was one of several races in the country between two female candidates, but these two candidates provided a clear choice for the Maryland electorate. Linda Chavez is a firm supporter of President Reagan's policies and has never held elected office. Mikulski, who was thought by some observers to be too liberal to be elected to the Senate, ran on her liberal record and her experience.[20] CBS exit polls indicated that she was supported by 58 percent of men and 64 percent of women, with 88 percent of blacks voting for her.

While Mikulski ran against three popular men in the Democratic primary, she had very strong support in Baltimore and its suburbs, and was ahead in the polls throughout the race.[21] She won the September primary comfortably. In the 1986 general election she had the advantages of statewide name recognition and the fact that she was running for a vacant seat.

Mikulski and other female candidates for Congress in 1986 also were aided by increased sophistication on the part of organized women throughout the country. One of the perennial problems of female candidates has been an inability to tap traditional sources of funding, but this is changing. The Women's Campaign Fund hoped to contribute $450,000 to women's campaigns in 1986. A new organization, EMILY's (Early Money Is Like Yeast), is dedicated to helping elect Democratic women to the Senate. As of June 1986 EMILY's had raised $168,000 for Mikulski and Harriet Woods of Missouri. This aid, the friendship of popular Democrats like Senator Kennedy for whom she campaigned vigorously in 1980, her record in the House, and the great asset of her personality made the odds more than even than she would advance to the Senate.

Mikulski has been called "the congressional champion of Baltimore's blue collar grit."[22] She has remained loyal to her roots even as her career took her further than her ancestors could have hoped a Polish woman could go in the United States. She is a feminist with strong support from working-class men, a liberal who didn't back down in conservative times. She has proven that the ethnic American woman can earn her way into that most exclusive of clubs, the Senate of the United States.

Notes

1. *Washington Post,* August 10, 1980.

2. Quoted in David S. Broder, *Changing the Guard* (New York: Simon and Schuster, 1980), 149.

3. *Washington Post,* August 10, 1980.

4. For good discussions of the development of Mikulski's philosophy, see Broder, *Changing the Guard,* 148–152, and the *Washington Post,* April 5, 1986.

5. Barbara Mikulski, "Who Speaks for Ethnic America?" *New York Times,* September 29, 1970.

6. Barbara Mikulski, "Introduction," in Nancy Seifer, *Absent from the Majority: Working Class Women in America* (New York: American Jewish Committee, c. 1973), viii–x.

7. Barbara Mikulski, "Women in Action" (A speech delivered at a meeting of Catholic sisters, Emmanuel College, Boston, MA, 1981).

8. Ibid.

9. Broder's account of the highway issue is one of the best (*Changing the Guard,* 150).

10. Quoted in ibid.

11. Mikulski, "Women in Action."

12. Quoted in "Barbara Mikulski for the U.S. Senate," *EMILY's List* (Washington, D.C.: February 1986).

13. Barbara Mikulski, "Deficits as Opportunities," *Christian Science Monitor,* January 15, 1985.

14. Barbara Mikulski, Letter to the Editor, *Washington Post,* April 7, 1982.

15. "Opponents Rewrite Unisex Insurance Bill," *Congressional Quarterly,* March 31, 1984, 42, 707.

16. Ibid., 707.

17. Mikulski, "Women in Action."

18. Ibid.

19. Ibid.

20. *New York Times,* November 5, 1986.

21. *New York Times,* June 15, 1986.

22. *Washington Post,* August 10, 1980.

Sandra Day O'Connor: Myra Bradwell's Revenge

ORMA LINFORD

The natural and proper timidity and delicacy which belongs to the female sex evidently unfits it for many of the occupations of civil life. . . . Incompetent fully to perform the duties and trusts that belong to the office of attorney and counsellor. . . . [The] paramount destiny and mission of woman are to fill the noble and benign offices of wife and mother. This is the law of the Creator.

Myra Bradwell *v.* State of Illinois (1873)

With this judicial adaptation of nineteenth-century male chauvinism, concurring Justice Joseph B. Bradley, in the first sex discrimination case heard by the U.S. Supreme Court, dismissed Myra Bradwell's claim that the U.S. Constitution protected her right to practice law and prohibited the state of Illinois from denying her admission to the bar.[1] I have no doubt that on September 25, 1981, an observant tourist on a sightseeing visit to the Supreme Court building, looking at a portrait of that 1873 court, at a certain hour would have seen a wince on Bradley's face: that was the day that Sandra Day O'Connor took the oath of office as the first woman to be appointed to the U.S. Supreme Court.

A President Looks For a Justice

In one sense the appointment of Sandra Day O'Connor to the Court was ironic: the most inherently conservative of the three branches of government, the judiciary seemed the most unlikely to be the first to surrender its highest office to a woman. After all, in 1981, only 5 percent of the nation's judges were women; women accounted for only 2 percent of the partners in the fifty largest law firms; in the law schools, only 5 percent of full professors were women; no state bar association had elected a woman as president; and no woman had ever served on the Board of Governors of the American Bar Association. As recently as 1970, only 8.5 percent of the students in law school were women, and women constituted fewer than 3 percent of the practicing attorneys. The numbers had improved by the time O'Connor was appointed, but the increase had no impact on the pool of candidates available to President Ronald Reagan when he went looking for a replacement for the retiring Justice Potter Stewart.[2]

Furthermore, Ronald Reagan seemed an unlikely champion of women. Although he expressed routinely his support for women's movement toward equality, his actions did not match his words. He was the first presidential candidate in recent memory to run on a platform that excluded the Equal Rights Amendment, and he appointed as solicitor general a Brigham Young University Mormon law school professor who had authored a book urging defeat of the ERA. Candidate Reagan was an uncompromising enemy of women's right to choose abortions, and his 1984 platform would include a plank proposing that federal judicial appointees be screened for commitment to "the sanctity of human life"—a provision universally interpreted as a promise to appoint judges only if they opposed abortion. Just 10 percent of his appointments to the highest positions in the executive branch had been women. Perhaps most significantly, while his predecessor Jimmy Carter had selected women for 19.6 percent of his appointments to the courts of appeals and 14.1 percent of his appointees to the district courts were women, Reagan's first round of judicial appointments included no women to the court of appeals, and women were only 4.3 percent of his appointees to the district courts.[3]

Life Before Ronald Reagan

Sandra Day O'Connor was born on March 26, 1930, the eldest child of Harry and Ada May Day. In a sense, young Sandra grew up in two different worlds. She was born in a hospital in El Paso, Texas, because the remote area in which her parents lived had no medical facilities—and, for a time, no running water or electricity. She would return to El Paso to receive her primary and secondary education because her parents found the local schools inadequate. But she spent her early childhood years and summer vacations on the cattle ranch called the Lazy B operated by her parents on 260 acres astride the New Mexico–Arizona border. Like most farm kids—male and female—she did her share of manual labor and learned to drive a truck well before she was old enough to get a driver's license. The other part of the time she lived with her grandmother in El Paso, where she attended a private elementary school and later a public high school. As a result, she received the quality schooling available in an urban area, while at the same time she learned the self-sufficiency skills required by ranch life in the desert country of the U.S. Southwest.

Her father's dreams were realized when she entered Stanford University in 1947 (he had wanted to attend Stanford). She graduated magna cum laude in 1950 and went on to Stanford Law School, where she received her law degree in 1952. She had completed the usual seven years of work in an impressively short five years. That same year she married a law school classmate John Jay O'Connor III. She served as deputy county attorney in San Mateo County, California, from 1952 to 1953. When her husband entered military service and was sent to Germany, she went with him and got a job as a civilian attorney for the army in Frankfurt from 1954 to 1957. After his discharge, they moved to Arizona, and O'Connor opened up a neighborhood law office with a partner and was engaged in private practice from 1958 to 1960. She took five years off to raise three sons. In 1965, Sandra Day O'Connor, who had not been exactly idle, really got down to business.

She served as an assistant attorney general of Arizona from 1965 to 1969. She was appointed to fill a vacancy in the senate in 1969 and was reelected twice to two-year terms, serving as majority leader in her last term. In 1975 she was elected to the Maricopa County Superior Court, which served Phoenix, and in 1979, Governor Bruce Babbit appointed her to the Arizona Court of Appeals, where, two years later, Ronald Reagan found her.[4]

Her Qualifications

Neither the Constitution nor federal statutes prescribe qualifications for Supreme Court justices, or for lower federal court judges for that matter. Only custom requires a federal judge to have a law degree. However, that is not the only requirement that custom and practice dictate. As Henry Abraham pointed out, a prospective justice must be "politically 'available' *and* acceptable to the executive, legislative, and private forces that . . . constitute the powers-that-be which underlie the paths of selection, nomination, and appointment."[5] On the whole, the 101 justices who preceded O'Connor had amazingly little prior judicial experience—of the 28 men appointed in the fifty years before her appointment, half had no prior judicial experience and half of those who did had five years or fewer on the bench. The Court being the singular and unique institution that it is, other qualities are more important. In the words of members of the Court themselves, a justice must be a "philosopher, historian, and prophet" and must possess "imagination, inordinate patience, poetic sensibilities . . . [and] antennae registering feeling and judgment beyond logical, let alone quantitative proof."[6] A justice must be a thinker more than a technician.

The first woman on the federal bench was Genevieve R. Cline, appointed by President Calvin Coolidge in 1928 to the U.S. Customs Court. The first woman to serve on a federal appellate court was Florence Allen, who was appointed to the Court of Appeals for the Sixth Circuit in 1934 by President Franklin Delano Roosevelt.[7] When Sandra Day O'Connor was appointed, there were just forty-four women on the courts of appeals and district courts.[8]

When Ronald Reagan went shopping for Potter Stewart's replacement, what was he looking for? Abraham has identified four kinds of influences on a president's choice: (1) objective merit, (2) personal friendship, (3) political and ideological compatibility, and (4) balance of representation on the Court.[9]

Merit

With regard to merit, there was much in Sandra Day O'Connor's background to recommend her. Her life had been devoted to public service. She had served in all three branches of government on the state level. She had been a county attorney in California and assistant attorney general in Arizona; she had spent more than six years in the Arizona legislature, the last three as majority leader of the Senate; and she had been a county judge before her appointment to the Arizona Court of Appeals. She had even spent some time with the military—as a civilian lawyer while her husband served a hitch in the army. She also knew what the private practice of law was about; she and a partner had operated a small neighborhood law office in Maryvale, Arizona.

The list of public activities on her official biographical data sheet reveals work with a constellation of civic, professional, and community organizations and causes, large and small, ranging from the Board of Trustees of Stanford University to the Soroptomist Club of Phoenix, from the Arizona Criminal Code Commission to the Maricopa County Juvenile Detention Home Visiting Board, and from the National Conference of Christians and Jews to the Board of Junior Achievement.[10]

Her academic credentials were sterling. A *magna cum laude* graduate of Stanford, she graduated third in her class at Stanford Law School. She had written for scholarly journals.

In determining whether she possessed the right "temperament," the President had reports of capacity for hard work, solid and methodical performance under pressure, mental toughness, and almost legendary serenity. She had impressed state senate colleagues with her conscientious and systematic preparation and equanimity. Lawyers who had practiced before her reported that she would tolerate nothing less than their best effort in competence, professionalism, and good manners.

On a personal level, she had a solid marriage with a man who shared her commitment to public life. She had reared three children. She was an athlete, with a respectable game of tennis and familiarity with ski hills on both sides of the Continental Divide. Friends said she was a good dancer, a good cook, and gave a good party.[11] In other words, Sandra Day O'Connor "had it all."

Friendship

Although she was not a close friend of the president, she had close friends who were. She had maintained her California connections, which served her well with a president whose own California connections are well known. Arizona Senator Barry Goldwater used his personal as well as political influence on her behalf. Justice William Rehnquist, a law review classmate at Stanford and longtime friend, was reported to have given her strong endorsement. Her case had been made well before she went to the White House for the formal interview, which she describes as "not very long."

Philosophy

As far as her judicial philosophy was concerned, she was almost perfect. She was a Republican, an *active* member of the president's own party. If people who have views about the role of the federal judiciary can be divided into two schools of thought —activists and passivists—she was clearly in the latter. She was a judge who would act in accordance with "judicial self-restraint," and that was the kind of judge the President wanted.

Judicial self-restraint can be described best in negative terms. To list its axioms is to make a catalogue of "shall nots." According to judicial self-restraint, even where federal courts have jurisdiction, meaning the power to hear and decide cases, judges should not do certain things. They should take care not to intrude upon the prerogatives of the legislative and executive branches—courts should not "make policy." They should not interfere with the states' exercise of their reserved powers—federal courts should respect the efforts of the states to solve public problems. They should not substitute their judgment for the judgments of state courts in cases where actions of states come under scrutiny of the federal courts. Other rules require refusing to hear cases where the parties lack "standing to sue"; the parties have not "exhausted" administrative or state "remedies"; issues are not "ripe" for adjudication; or the parties are asking the Court to decide "hypothetical" questions or give "advisory opinions." These rules lack precision, and there are frequent close calls, but the evidence—her appellate court opinions, legislative voting record, and public statements and writings —indicated that Judge O'Connor could be trusted to keep the faith.

Among those who mattered, only the extremists on the far right did not give her a clean bill of ideological health—they scoured her voting record in the Arizona legislature and found suggestions that she had supported the right to abortion and the ERA. As it turned out, the record was ambiguous.[12] As far as the general public was concerned, her nomination was a definite hit. A Gallup poll in August 1981 found that 69 percent of Americans considered her qualified for the job; only 4 percent thought that she was not qualified.[13]

Balance of Representation

In achieving the final objective—balance of representation on the Court— Ronald Reagan, of course, would make history. Regional, religious, and racial considerations have motivated Court appointments in the past. Although Justice Rehnquist's roots are in Arizona, he did not reside there when he was appointed, so O'Connor would formally correct the underrepresentation of the western part of the country. Although Justice William Brennan occupies the "Catholic seat" on the Court, there has not been anyone in the "Jewish seat" since Abe Fortas resigned, so it could be argued that in recent times religion has not been an important factor. When Lyndon Johnson appointed Justice Thurgood Marshall in 1967, a "black seat" was created.

While women were making steady progress toward equality in all fields, the absence of a female justice became increasingly unacceptable in the 1970s. Presidential candidates from the 1972 election on routinely promised the appointment of a woman to the Court, and when President Gerald Ford had to find a successor to William O. Douglas, several women's names actually circulated.

Despite what looked like impressive credentials, Sandra Day O'Connor hardly had national name recognition. She was an obscure state judge—not even on the highest court of the state. On the other hand, men with more modest credentials have been nominated in the past. O'Connor herself is unequivocal. When asked recently whether she thought it was the fact that she was a woman that got her the nomination, she said without hesitation and with certainty, "Why, I *do*. I'm sure that was the main thing."[14]

After the clear indication that Reagan gave during his campaign that he wanted to appoint a woman to the Court, O'Connor thinks that the pool of candidates he immediately turned to were Republican female judges, and "there aren't many women judges in the country to begin with, and there are even fewer Republican women judges." She refuses to speculate about the suggestion that because the President was committed to appointing a woman, the standards for selection were lower than they would have been if he had been considering men as well. "I'm not going to rate myself. . . . I hope not [that he didn't lower the standards]. That's for others to say, not me."

There was still another thread in all this.

> I would imagine that my age had something to do with it. If you're going to make an appointment to the Court, I'm not sure that you want to put someone on who is so old that they can only serve a brief time. Nor do you want to appoint someone who is so young that they lack experience. That pretty much confines you to someone in the middle years, and I doubt that there were very many women Republican judges in their middle years from which he could make a selection.

So: gender, party, judicial experience, and age were the four central factors in O'Connor's nomination, with gender being the determinative factor. Once it was decided that it was to be a woman, the other factors pointed very quickly to a particular woman—Sandra Day O'Connor.

But How Would She Be on Women's Issues?

With a variety of issues affecting women likely to come before the Court, feminists were of two minds. They were enthusiastic about the fact that a woman had been appointed, but she was a judicial and political conservative. To know some things about her life experience would have been to know something about how she would behave on the Court.

Contact With Sex Discrimination

Justice O'Connor feels that she personally was the victim of sex discrimination at only one point in her life—when, looking for her first jobs, initially in California and later in Arizona, no major law firm would hire her because she was a woman. She was offered positions as a legal secretary, but prospective employers explained that they did not hire women as attorneys.

During her grade school and high school years, she lived with her grandmother, a strong, independent woman who clearly passed on those characteristics to her granddaughter. O'Connor says that while she was growing up, she was given "*enormous* freedom" and that her grandmother "thought anything I wanted to do was fine, and there wasn't anything I *couldn't* do as far as she was concerned."

She felt no discrimination in law school. "I always competed [with male students], and I did not feel hassled. I thought I was accepted. I got good assignments on the law review, and my professors treated me very nicely."

Her professors provided her with no assistance in finding a job after graduation, but she says that they gave no help to anyone else. She apparently found no evidence of an "old boys" network.

When she was a trial attorney, she reports that judges and colleagues treated her no differently than they treated male lawyers, despite the fact that the women lawyers in Phoenix were so few that when they had lunch together, they "could all sit at a fairly small table."

Once she discovered that the private sector was closed to her, she found a series of positions in the public sector, where, she maintains, her gender was never a handicap. "Once I could get my foot in the door, I was always able to develop a job or a position that I thought was pleasing and one in which I was happily accepted by my peers and colleagues."

In addition to her grandmother, she had a strong role model in Lorna Lockwood, who would become the first woman to serve as the chief justice of a state supreme court. "She was a woman whose life in many ways preceded mine. She grew up in a rural area, was an assistant attorney general, a state legislator, a trial court judge, and later an appellate court judge. She was always interested in all of the women lawyers, gave generously of her time and attention. Her experience in Arizona certainly made it easier for me." So, Sandra Day O'Connor had seen a woman make it—and make it *big* —in a man's world.

Experience in State Government

The fact that O'Connor served as a state legislator and state judge—both trial and appellate—helped shape her views about the kind of role that the Supreme Court should play in the U.S. political system. She worked very hard, and saw colleagues work very hard, on significant matters of public policy, and she learned respect for the products of the legislative process. As a result, she thinks that the Supreme Court should pay deference to legislative bodies. As a state judge, she saw colleagues arrive at sound decisions, ensure that justice was dispensed, and make good law. Consequently, she does not accept the notion that federal judges are somehow better than state judges and thinks that the Supreme Court should be reluctant to substitute its judgment for that of state courts. These are two important axioms of judicial self-restraint and could determine her position in cases where legislatures or state courts have made decisions involving women's issues.

The Constitution, Stare Decisis, and Women

While she was in the state senate, the Arizona legislature debated the ratification of the Equal Rights Amendment,[15] and she describes the lobbying by its proponents and opponents as something close to a siege. "We would get *floods* of mail on both sides of the issue. There was *great* pressure on every single member of the legislature, by both sides." She attributes the defeat of the ERA to the *depth* and *intensity* of the divisions it caused in the country rather than to the *size* of the opposition or the *merits* of its arguments. "It is clear that women throughout the country were themselves divided, and that division went right down to the grass-roots level. When that kind of *heated* confrontation emerges over any issue, it makes the likelihood of affirmative legislative action greatly reduced." Her position on the Equal Rights Amendment itself is ambiguous. On the other hand, maybe it does not matter whether she thought it was a good idea as policy because she gives the clear impression that she does think that it is *not* a good idea to enact policy when the debate about it has provoked such deep and emotional differences.

Given the absence of the ERA, women—and men as well—have been forced to depend for constitutional protection against sex discrimination on Supreme Court interpretation of the provisions that forbid state and federal governments to deny any person "the equal protection of the laws."[16] The standards of equal protection analysis vary, and the one that the Court selects virtually determines the outcome of a case. The Court has applied a very demanding standard in cases involving race discrimination. It has found distinctions based upon race to be inherently "suspect classifications," which require proof of a "compelling governmental interest" to sustain them, and subjects governmental justifications to "strict judicial scrutiny."[17] Given the rigor of the standard it can be argued that no racial classification could survive judicial examination under the equal protection clause.

The Court, however, has refused to declare classifications based upon sex to be suspect, and consequently, applies a less rigorous test. The governmental interest only has to be "important," and the Court will give just plain "scrutiny" to such governmental action. The Court's inquiry simply requires that the action bear a "close and substantial relationship" to the governmental interest.[18] As a result of the relaxed standard, there have been several instances where the Court has upheld governmental action that treats men and women differently—for example, the male-only draft.[19]

It should be noted that there is a third standard of review according to which the Court requires only that the governmental action have a "reasonable (or 'rational') basis." This is the test used to determine the constitutionality of garden-variety classifications, like tax laws or zoning ordinances, and is not a demanding standard.[20]

O'Connor refuses to say whether she thinks the Court adopted the correct standard for sex discrimination cases, but knowing that she places great value on precedent suggests which standard she will obey. But even independent of *stare decisis* (Latin for "let the decision stand"),[21] it is significant that she explains the different judicial treatment of race and sex in historical terms. "The Thirteenth, Fourteenth, and Fifteenth Amendments were adopted in direct response to the Civil War and to the plight of *race-based* discrimination. The application of those amendments, and thus the equal protection clause, to gender-based discrimination came later, *much* later, and the Court simply employed a different test."

Another interesting aspect to all of this is that her subscription to the historical approach to interpreting the equal protection clause sits side by side with her belief, stated in very strong terms, that the Court has a special responsibility to protect persons who cannot prevail in the political process. Buying into the historical explanation overlooks the facts that sex, like race, is an immutable characteristic and that women and blacks share similar legacies marked by stereotyping, discrimination, and political powerlessness. But, then again, it should be remembered that she recognizes none of this in her own experience.

On the Court

O'Connor has now served more than five years on the Court. Her apprenticeship can be considered over, and her record is sufficient for at least some tentative conclusions. Did the president get what he thought he was getting? It seems fairly clear that he did. The discussion that follows analyzes her performance in three ways: first, some general observations on what her voting record indicates about her general approach to the role of the Court in the U.S. political system; second, how she has voted on cases involving civil rights and liberties in general; and third, a review of her record in cases that affect, either directly or by analogy, women's issues.

Basic Approaches

To begin with, it ought to be noted that she usually voted on the same side as former Chief Justice Burger and Chief Justice Rehnquist, who were identified as the conservative wing of the Court, but usually they deserted her when she voted in favor of women's rights.[22] There are Supreme Court watchers who would make out a gradual movement toward more independence on O'Connor's part, and this view received encouragement from the 1985–1986 term of Court, when she split from Burger and Rehnquist in a few high-profile cases. A study of the sixty-nine "polarized" cases—cases in which Burger and Rehnquist voted together and took a different position than Brennan and Marshall, the liberal wing of the Court—reveals that O'Connor voted against Burger and Rehnquist in sixteen of the sixty-nine cases. Be this as it may, fifty-three out of sixty-nine is still a high percentage of agreement, and she dissented from only one opinion each *written* by Burger and Rehnquist.[23] Only time will tell whether the rumors of independence have any substance.

When the issue is not which way the Court will decide a case or a question, but whether it should hear it in the first place, and the justices disagree, she is much more likely than not to vote against reaching the merits, by dismissing it, for example, for want of jurisdiction or lack of "standing to sue."[24] (In order to establish "standing to sue," a litigant must establish a concrete, immediate, and personal interest in the outcome of the case.) In a case that requires a judgment on whether an administrative agency has acted unconstitutionally or illegally, the odds are very good that she will uphold the agency action.[25] If the Court is asked to invalidate an action of a state legislature or the state executive branch, she is more likely than not to vote in the state's favor.[26] In a case in which the Court is asked to review the findings and conclusions of the highest court in the state, she usually votes to accept them.[27]

Individual Rights and Liberties

In the area of constitutionally protected rights and liberties, her position, to a great extent, depends on what right or liberty is at issue. In procedural due process cases, a criminal defendant can expect little comfort from Justice O'Connor—she has voted about five times more often to uphold a conviction than to reverse it. In cases involving the substantive liberties of conscience, expression, and association, the reviews are mixed. Although she has voted to sustain government action challenged on these grounds more often than not,[28] she has contributed to significant First Amendment victories.[29] Where property interests under the due process clauses of the Constitution have been involved, she usually votes against the government action and to sustain the property rights.[30]

American Indians usually have an even chance with her, but she votes against claims of aliens—for example, due process hearings before deportation[31] or access to state-funded education.[32] She has voted against students by upholding warrantless searches of a college dormitory room[33] and of a high school student's handbag.[34]

In applying the federal statute that provides for the award of attorney's fees in civil rights suits, O'Connor has consistently agreed that fees should be awarded only for work done on legal arguments that are successful.[35] She has also voted to grant immunity from suit to certain government officials, thus eliminating a potential defendant in civil rights actions.[36]

Equal Protection and Other Women's Rights Cases

In cases involving race, she agrees with the discrimination claim in roughly half the cases. In sex discrimination cases, she has much more often voted in favor of the claimant—but there are very important exceptions.

Her posture in two kinds of civil rights cases involving race is of interest because they involve matters of general equal protection principle. In the Memphis firefighters case,[37] she joined four other justices in ruling that a federal district court could *not* order the city to maintain a certain percentage of black employees when it meant layoffs of white employees with more seniority. She also added a separate concurring opinion in which she emphasized that she thought that the federal statute that prohibits employers from discriminating on the basis of race protects the rights of *white male* employees. The Memphis case was widely interpreted as the beginning of the end for affirmative action. Another case was a suit brought by black and Hispanic police officers in New York City, where she wrote a concurring opinion insisting that proof of *intent* to discriminate was essential to a valid claim under a federal civil rights statute—proof of discriminatory *effect* is not enough.[38]

Sex Discrimination   During her first term on the Court, she participated in six pertinent cases. First, she joined the Court in removing a jurisdictional barrier to a suit brought by female flight attendants against Trans World Airlines that challenged TWA's policy of grounding all female flight attendants who became mothers while permitting male counterparts who became fathers to continue flying.[39] She also voted to uphold administrative regulations prohibiting federally funded education programs from discriminating on the basis of sex in employment.[40] Next, joining an opinion written by Justice Marshall, she helped clear the way for a female employee to sue a Florida state university for race and sex discrimination, but not without a reminder of judicial self-restraint in her separate concurring opinion.[41]

In two other cases, her sympathies were not with the female complainants. She joined the Court's ruling against the employees of American Tobacco Company, who claimed race and sex discrimination under federal civil rights law,[42] and she wrote for the Court to cancel a lower federal court's award of back pay to female employees of Ford Motor Company.[43]

In the last case, writing for the Court, she held invalid the policy of a state-supported university excluding males from its school of nursing. *Mississippi University for Women v. Hogan*[44] is an important case because she explained the equal protection standard that she will apply in sex discrimination cases. It is also significant because she disagreed sharply with her most consistent judicial soulmates, Burger and Rehnquist, who both wrote dissenting opinions. There was no surprise in *Hogan*. She followed precedent and applied the intermediate standard of review. It was, however, a strong restatement, and the kind of examination that she gave to the state's announced interests did not fall much short of "strict scrutiny." In a careful footnote, she firmly rejected the suggestion made by Justice Powell, in his separate concurring opinion, that a less rigorous standard of review could be applied. Even though the case involved unfair treatment of males, she made it clear that the equal protection test cuts both ways. "It must be applied free of fixed notions concerning the roles and abilities of males and females."[45] She gave the footnote to Myra Bradwell.

There were three cases during the 1982–1983 term. She voted with the majority in holding that an employer's health plan that gave less pregnancy coverage to the spouses of male employees than it gave to female employees violated the Pregnancy Discrimination Act.[46] But the following week she agreed with the Court when it held that the father of an illegitimate child was not entitled to be notified of its adoption, although the state gave that right to the mother.[47] Finally, she agreed that a federal civil rights law was violated by an Arizona retirement plan that provided lower monthly annuity payments for state employees who were women, but then she turned around and wrote a concurring opinion in support of granting only prospective relief.[48]

Midway through the 1983–1984 term, O'Connor helped deliver a serious blow to women's equality in education. *Grove City College v. Bell*[49] ruled that the federal statute that prohibits sex discrimination in any education program requires termination of federal funding for only the specific *part* of the program in which discrimination was found, not for the entire institution. In another case, she wrote a partially concurring opinion in support of the enforcement of an Employment Opportunity Commission subpoena, but she complained about what she considered lack of notice to the defendant, Shell Oil Company.[50] Next, she joined a unanimous Court in upholding a federal statute providing a five-year extension of a gender-based classification for determining Social Security benefits that the Court had previously held unconstitutional. Because wage earners had depended upon the statute in making their retirement plans, Congress could protect them from the damaging effects of that previous decision—an "important governmental interest."[51]

Later that month, she joined a plurality *per curiam* opinion that held that a woman employee had forfeited the right to sue her former employer because she had not filed her complaint in accordance with the statute of limitations.[52] In a fourth case, she was a member of a unanimous Court that ruled that Florida could not take custody of a child away from a mother and give it to the father, when the mother, who was Caucasian, married a black man.[53]

In *Hishon v. King and Spaulding,*[54] a unanimous Court declared that a law firm violated federal civil rights law when it fired a woman lawyer who had been told when she was hired as an associate that she could expect to become a partner, although male associates had been made partners. The brethren, no doubt, were mindful of their "sister's" experience. Finally, the Court told the U.S. Jaycees that their freedoms of expression and association were not violated when Minnesota interpreted its human rights statute to prohibit the organization from excluding women. O'Connor joined in the judgment and wrote a separate concurring opinion.[55]

The 1984–1985 term provided only one significant sex discrimination case, and O'Connor agreed with the Court's finding for a woman whose application for city recreation director was rejected in favor of a less-experienced, less well-qualified man.[56]

The 1985–1986 term produced the Court's first opinion involving sexual harassment as a violation of federal civil rights legislation.[57] All nine justices agreed that a female bank employee was the victim of sex discrimination because her supervisor created an environment of intimidation in the workplace with his unwelcome sexual advances, regardless of the facts that she had not been forced against her will to submit to his attentions and that there was no economic quid pro quo. However, six justices agreed that employers are *not* always liable for sexual harassment of employees by their supervisors, and O'Connor was one of the six.

Earlier, O'Connor was among the majority when the Court held that Social Security legislation granting survivor's benefits to a wage earner's *widowed* but remarried spouse, but not to a remarried surviving spouse who had *divorced* him, was not a violation of equal protection.[58]

O'Connor was also in the majority in a 5-4 decision refusing to review a lower federal court ruling that the application of a state statute prohibiting sex discrimination to a private school violated the constitutional protection of freedom of religion.[59]

In three decisions announced toward the end of the term, the Court stood up to the Reagan administration's full-tilt assault on affirmative action, and although these decisions involved race, not sex, the principles involved have general application.[60] O'Connor joined five other justices in two cases approving court orders requiring preferential treatment of nonwhites who are not actual victims of discrimination and directing a union to meet membership goals and establish a fund to be used to remedy discrimination. She did balk a bit, however—in both cases, she added concurring opinions expressing objections and separating herself from certain parts of the majority opinions. She joined a different, smaller majority to invalidate a third affirmative action program, but again added a concurring opinion that made it clear that she was not deserting race-conscious remedies for discrimination—in fact, significantly for women, she recognized as a permissible governmental interest the provision of "role models."

Abortion Under questioning during her confirmation hearings, she told the Senate that she was personally opposed to abortion, but that it would be improper for her to speculate about constitutional and legal issues that might come before her as a member of the Court in the future. The fact that some senators were left unsatisfied by her answers presented no threat to her confirmation.[61] As it turned out, the Moral Majority had nothing to worry about.

As the only member of the Court to have personal experience with childbearing, how she would vote on cases involving it was of great interest to almost everyone. Not until her second year did the Court accept more abortion cases for full argument. There were three in all, the most important of which involved an Akron, Ohio, ordinance that can best be characterized as an expression of "massive resistance" to the line of cases, which began with *Roe v. Wade*[62] in 1973, upholding the constitutional right of a woman to decide whether or not to terminate her pregnancy.

The Court has measured the constitutionality of legislation regulating abortion in accordance with a three-part formula that divides a pregnancy into three trimesters and defines the legislative power differently in each. During the first three months, when abortion is relatively safe, the right of the woman to choose takes precedence and the state cannot impose special regulations; after the third month, the state can regulate, but only if the regulation relates to the state's interest in maternal health; and after the sixth month, when the fetus can theoretically survive outside the mother's body, the state's interest in potential life supports the prohibition of all abortions, except to preserve the mother's life and health.

The Akron ordinance contained seventeen different provisions "regulating" abortion, each designed to discourage it or make it more difficult to obtain. The substantive provisions were introduced by several "findings," one of which "found" that human life begins with the union of sperm and egg. When the case reached the Court, there were just five sections at issue— requirements of hospitalization, informed consent, parental consent, a waiting period, and the humane disposal of fetal remains. In *City of Akron v. Akron Center for Reproductive Health*,[63] the Court struck down all five.

O'Connor, writing for White and Rehnquist, authored the dissent. She began by rejecting the approach that has consistently governed the Court's analysis of legislation regulating abortion since 1973. She argued that technological advances have made, and will continue to make, the Court's three-part formula obsolete. The safety of second trimester abortions has increased dramatically, she said, so that if a state's power is measured by its interest in the mother's health, regulation may be prohibited until well after the third month; likewise, medical advances have made, and will continue to make, the possibility of the fetus living outside the mother's body much earlier than six months. "Just as improvements in medical technology inevitably will move *forward* the point at which the State may regulate for reasons of maternal health, different technological improvements will move *backward* the point of viability at which the State may proscribe abortions except when necessary to preserve the life and health of the mother."[64] She found it hard to believe that the Constitution requires legislatures to revise their laws every time the American College of Obstetricians and Gynecologists revises its standards as to what is the appropriate medical procedure in this area.

Instead of "due process by trimester," she would apply a single standard to determine the constitutionality of legislation, regardless of what stage of pregnancy was being regulated. The Court should ask, she insisted, whether the regulation was "unduly burdensome," and given that yardstick, none of the Akron provisions imposed an "undue burden" on the woman's right of choice. It ought to be pointed out that the "undue burden" test was used in the abortion funding cases, which raised an entirely different set of legal issues.

Her opinion does not state flatly that she thinks that legislative bodies *do* have the power that *Roe* declared unconstitutional, but she gave voice to her belief that "the state's interest in protecting potential human life exists *throughout* the pregnancy" and argued for a substantial relaxation of the demanding "strict scrutiny" rule that the Court has said it must apply in these cases.[65] Also, her opinion was liberally sprinkled with approving references to "reasonable" and "rational" as descriptions of the appropriate measure of state interest required, as contrasted with the Court's overall consistent demand for proof of a "compelling" interest. Clearly, she would give legislatures a far wider berth in the regulation of abortions.

In the second case, where the Court struck down a Missouri statute requiring second trimester abortions to be performed in hospitals, she again wrote in dissent.[66] In the third case she wrote an opinion approving a Virginia requirement that second trimester abortions be performed in licensed clinics.[67] She repeated her view of the proper constitutional recipe—neither statute constituted an "undue burden" on the constitutional right of women.

The 1985–1986 term provided one abortion case, in which O'Connor again made pro-choice advocates nervous by dissenting from a decision declaring unconstitutional four provisions of a Pennsylvania abortion control act. Although her dissenting opinion would have given a victory to those who deny any constitutional right to abortion, it serves, in a perverse way, as a sort of damage control: first, she does not join the dissenting opinions of Burger, White, or Rehnquist, who ask for a reexamination of *Roe v. Wade,* and second, she attacks the Court on matters of procedure, rather than substance.[68]

The Bottom Line

President Dwight Eisenhower once said that his appointment of Earl Warren as chief justice in 1953 was "the worst damn fool mistake I ever made,"[69] and Richard Nixon has been given reason to wonder about Justice Harry Blackmun. Sandra Day O'Connor, on the other hand, is almost exactly what Ronald Reagan ordered. The reviews of her record on women's issues are mixed. She has managed to satisfy on some issues and antagonize on others almost everyone, and she is proof that a woman on the bench is not a guarantee of decisions in favor of women's rights. Two obvious but important facts should not be overlooked. First, as the youngest member of an aging Court, Sandra Day O'Connor will be with us for a long time. On the other hand, in view of the men who have been mentioned in recent years as candidates for Supreme Court justices, feminists could have fared much worse—and probably will. In any event, Myra Bradwell would be pleased that Sandra Day O'Connor is there at all.

Notes

1. Bradwell v. Illinois, 83 U.S. 130 (1873).

2. Library of Congress (Telephone, April 4, 1985); *Time,* July 20, 1981, 17.

3. *Time,* July 20, 1981, 8; *Congressional Quarterly* 39 (December 26, 1981):2560.

4. Sandra Day O'Connor, Biographical Data Sheet.

5. Henry Abraham, *The Judicial Process* (New York: Oxford University Press, 1986), 53.

6. Ibid., 55.

7. Ibid., 62.

8. Library of Congress (Telephone, April 4, 1985).

9. Abraham, *The Judicial Process,* 64.

10. Information for this section is taken from her official Biographical Data Sheet and the author's conversation with Justice O'Connor on January 24, 1986, in her office.

11. *Newsweek,* July 20, 1981, 16–19; *Time,* July 20, 1981, 8–19.

12. *Congressional Quarterly* 39 (July 11, 1981):1235; (September 12, 1981): 1731–1732; (September 26, 1981):1831; (October 31, 1981):2145.

13. *The Gallup Report,* no. 198 (August 1981):3–5. On the broader question of the idea of a woman on the Court, 86 percent approved.

14. Conversation with Justice O'Connor in her chambers on January 24, 1986. Hereafter, because all direct quotations from her in this chapter come from that conversation, they will not be footnoted.

15. Section 1. Equality of rights under the law shall not be denied or abridged by the United States or any state on account of sex. Section 2. The Congress shall have the power to enforce, by appropriate legislation, the provisions of this article. Section 3. This Amendment shall take effect two years after the date of ratification.

16. The Fourteenth Amendment applies this prohibition to the *states*; the Court has ruled that the Fifth Amendment due process clause contains an equal protection "component" that applies to the *federal* government.

17. For example, University of California Regents v. Bakke, 438 U.S. 265; 57 L.Ed.2d 750 (1978) (Per Powell, J.).

18. For example, Craig v. Boren, 429 U.S. 190; 50 L.Ed.2d 397 (1976).

19. Rostker v. Goldberg, 453 U.S. 57; 69 L.Ed.2d 478 (1981).

20. For example, United States Railroad Retirement Board v. Fritz, 449 U.S. 166; 66 L.Ed.2d 368 (1980).

21. *Stare decisis* refers to a judicial rule that binds the Court to apply legal principles that have been established in previous cases (precedents) with clearly similar facts, unless there is a very strong reason not to do so.

22. Chief Justice Burger resigned after the 1985–1986 term. Associate Justice Rehnquist was appointed to replace him as chief justice. Antonin Scalia, a judge on the Court of Appeals for the District of Columbia, was appointed to replace Rehnquist.

23. The National Law Journal, August 11, 1986, S-2.

24. For example, Allen v. Wright, U.S.; 82 L.Ed.2d 556 (1984) (O'Connor, J.). It is interesting to note that the *U.S. Reports* have traditionally announced the author of an opinion as "Mr. Justice _____"; now that a woman is on the bench the Mr. has been dropped, thus avoiding the painful decision of what to call her—Mrs., Ms., Madame, etc.

25. For example, Commissioner of Internal Revenue v. Tufts, 461 U.S. 300; 75 L.Ed.2d 863 (1983) (concurring, O'Connor, J.).

26. For example, Rice v. Rehner, 463 U.S. 714; 77 L.Ed.2d 961 (1983) (per O'Connor, J.).

27. For example, her dissent in Southland Corporation v. Keating, 465 U.S. 37; 79 L.Ed.2d 1 (1984) (per Burger, C. J.).

28. For example, Board of Education v. Pico, 457 U.S. 853; 73 L.Ed.2d 435 (1982) (dissenting, O'Connor, J.).

29. For example, Kolender v. Lawson, 461 U.S. 352; 75 L.Ed.2d 903 (1983) (per O'Connor, J.).

30. Ruckelshaus v. Monsanto, U.S.; 81 L.Ed.2d 815 (1984) (concur/dissent, O'Connor, J.).

31. For example, Immigration and Naturalization Service v. Lopez-Mendoza, U.S.; 82 L.Ed.2d 778 (1984) (per O'Connor, J.).

32. Pyler v. Doe, 457 U.S. 202; 72 L.Ed.2d 786 (1982) (dissenting, Burger, C. J.).

33. Washington v. Chrisman, 455 U.S. 1; 70 L.Ed.2d 778 (1982) (per Burger, C. J.).

34. New Jersey v. T.L.O., U.S.; 83 L.Ed.2d 720 (1985) (per White, J.).

35. For example, Ruckelshaus v. Sierra Club, 468 U.S. 680; 77 L.Ed.2d 938 (1983) (per Rehnquist, J.).

36. For example, Pennhurst State School v. Halderman, 465 U.S. 89; 79 L.Ed.2d 67 (1984) (per Powell, J.).

37. Firefighters v. Stotts, U.S.; 81 L.Ed.2d 483 (1984) (per White, J.).

38. Guardians Association v. Civil Service Commission of New York, 463 U.S. 582; 77 L.Ed.2d 866 (1983) (concurring, O'Connor, J.).

39. Zipes v. Trans World Airlines, 455 U.S. 385; 71 L.Ed.2d 234 (1982) (per White, J.).

40. North Haven Board of Education v. Bell, 456 U.S. 512; 72 L.Ed.2d 299 (1982) (per Blackman, J.).

41. Patsy v. Board of Regents, 457 U.S. 496; 73 L.Ed.2d 172 (1982).

42. American Tobacco Company v. Patterson, 456 U.S. 63; 71 L.Ed. 2d 748 (1982) (per White, J.).

43. Ford Motor Company v. Equal Employment Opportunity Commission, 458 U.S. 219; 73 L.Ed.2d 721 (1982).

44. 458 U.S. 718; 73 L.Ed.2d 1090 (1982).

45. 458 U.S. at 724-25; 73 L.Ed.2d at 725.

46. Newport News Shipbuilding and Dry Dock Company v. EEOC, 462 U.S. 699; 77 L.Ed.2d 89 (1983) (per Stevens, J.).

47. Lehr v. Robertson, 463 U.S. 248; 77 L.Ed.2d 614 (1983) (per Stevens, J.).

48. Arizona Governing Committee v. Norris, 463 U.S. 1073; 77 L.Ed.2d 1236 (1983) (*per curiam*). Another case decided during this term was not a discrimination case, but it affected women's rights as wives; the Court held that federal tax law authorized the sale of a delinquent male taxpayer's house despite the fact that his wife, who had a homestead interest in the house, owed none of the indebtedness. O'Connor joined a separate opinion written by Blackman concurring in part and dissenting in part. United States v. Rodgers, 461 U.S. 677; 76 L.Ed.2d 236 (1983) (per Brennan, J.).

49. Grove City College v. Bell, 465 U.S. 555; 79 L.Ed.2d 516 (1984) (per White, J.).

50. Equal Employment Opportunity Commission v. Shell Oil Company, U.S.; 80 L.Ed.2d 41 (1983) (per Marshall, J.).

51. Heckler v. Matthews, 465 U.S. 728; 79 L.Ed.2d 646 (1984) (per Brennan, J.).

52. Baldwin County Welcome Center v. Brown, U.S.; 80 L.Ed.2d 196 (1984).

53. Palmore v. Sidoti, U.S.; 80 L.Ed.2d 421 (1984).

54. U.S.; 81 L.Ed.2d 59 (1984).

55. Roberts v. United States Jaycees, U.S.; 82 L.Ed.2d 462 (1984) (per Brennan, J.). In a case that was decided on self-incrimination grounds, although it did involve a sex classification, O'Connor joined the Court in upholding the so-called Solomon Amendment, which denies federal financial assistance to college students who fail to register for the draft; only males are required to register. Selective Service v. Minnesota Public Interest Research Group, 468 U.S.; 82 L.Ed.2d (1984) (per Burger, C. J.).

56. Anderson v. Bessemer City, U.S.; 84 L.Ed.2d 518 (1985) (per White, J.).

57. Savings Bank v. Vison, U.S.; 91 L.Ed.2d 49 (1986).

58. Bowen v. Owens, U.S.; 90 L.Ed.2d 316 (1986).

59. Ohio Civil Rights Commission v. Dayton Schools, U.S.; 90 L.Ed.2d 512 (1986).

60. Sheet Metal Workers v. EEOC, U.S.; 92 L.Ed.2d 344 (1986); Firefighters v. Cleveland, U.S.; 92 L.Ed.2d 405 (1986); Wygant v. Jackson Board of Education, U.S.; 92 L.Ed.2d 260 (1986).

61. *Congressional Quarterly* 39, (July 11, 1981):1235.

62. 410 U.S. 113; 35 L.Ed.2d 147 (1973).

63. Akron v. Akron Center for Reproductive Health, 462 U.S. 416; 76 L.Ed.2d 687 (1983) (per Powell, J.).

64. 462 U.S., at 456; 76 L.Ed.2d, at 720.

65. 462 U.S., at 461; 76 L.Ed.2d, at 723.

66. Planned Parenthood v. Ashcroft, 462 U.S. 476; 76 L.Ed.2d 733 (1983) (per Powell, J.).

67. Simopoulos v. Virginia, 462 U.S. 506; 76 L.Ed.2d 755 (1983).

68. Thornburgh v. American College of Obstetricians and Gynecologists, U.S.; 90 L.Ed.2d 799 (1986). Although it did not affect women, Bowers v. Hardwick, U.S.; 92 L.Ed.2d 140 (1986), which upheld the application of a criminal sodomy law to activity between homosexuals in a private home, does have implications for the right of privacy.

69. Quoted in S. Sidney Ulmer, *Courts, Law and Judicial Processes* (New York: Free Press, 1981), 252.

The Unnamed
Political Woman

IRENE J. DABROWSKI

Historically, women have exerted their greatest political influence and have
demonstrated their leadership at the local level of politics, shaping public
policy in cities and communities as volunteers.[1] Elected national power, the
most visible layer of politics, has been the domain of men who have been
the presidents, vice presidents, and most of the senators, governors, representatives, and other prestigious officeholders formally chosen by the electorate. Volunteerism—that is, an exercise in the practical politics of participatory democracy that is at the same time devoid of salary and frequently
without official recognition—can be considered the "women's work" of
politics. Women who volunteer as organizers, coordinators, door-to-door
canvassers, project overseers, lobbyists, demonstrators, political party workers, and in a wide variety of other roles that are supportive of and even innovative to municipal institutions, human service delivery, and political
machines are generally taken for granted, and their names along with their
contributions remain anonymous.[2]

Feminist criticism of volunteer work, as presented in the writings of the
National Organization for Women (NOW), considers volunteerism, particularly service-oriented volunteer work, a sexist institution that robs women
of their potential economic resources and delegates them to the status of
second-class citizens.[3] Within the feminist perspective, however, the issue of
volunteer work does not lend itself to a single position but instead to numerous interpretations that vary with changing times and social needs. Betty
Friedan, the mother of the contemporary women's movement, in her recent
book *The Second Stage* urges feminists to rethink their earlier resistance to
volunteerism. Friedan claims that the present demands of the new equality
in combination with current political and economic realities require a committed response that she terms "human politics." According to the "human
politics" ethic, women and men together should share responsibility for sur-

vival in the interrelated spheres of family, community, and government. Friedan emphasizes an equal contribution by the sexes specifically in volunteer work in order to meet daily, practical needs and shape new systems of service for contemporary lifestyles. She expects that women and men will undertake the responsibility of volunteerism together as they become increasingly aware of their reliance upon communal amenities.[4] Similarly, futurist Alvin Toffler predicts the emergence of "anticipatory democracy" in the twenty-first century, a do-it-yourself approach to government in which problems are resolved by citizens themselves at local levels.[5]

Increasingly, in the face of government bureaucracy, volunteer/civic/special interest groups are theoretically acknowledged as important to urban governance, and they do in fact function as critical components of our political process. However, sociologists like Linda Christiansen-Ruffman contend that in our overall conceptions of government and participation, women's volunteer work is still very often regarded as separate and different from the real politics of men and therefore remains "secondary and unimportant."[6] The purpose of this chapter is to investigate selected aspects of women's volunteer work and thereby to show how typical U.S. women have been active political participants whose contributions are equivalent to those of men.

Early Volunteerism in Cities and Political Parties

The historical continuum of women's political activism in this country is reconstructed and comprehensively discussed by political scientist Marilyn Gittell and sociologist Teresa Shtob in *Signs,* a leading journal on women and culture.[7] The authors have discovered that in general "women who could not participate directly in the political life of the city historically used the voluntary association as a channel for their interests and energies."[8]

The inception of women's public involvement corresponds socially to the development of cities in the nineteenth century and politically to the Progressive Era in the early decades of the twentieth century when scores of primarily middle-class women organized campaigns directed at urban reform. It was in this era of urban reform movements that women mobilized their efforts against the morally disorganizing features of city life, such as gambling and prostitution, with the larger goal of reducing poverty.[9] Among the most prominent voluntary organizations of this era was the Women's Christian Temperance Union (WCTU), established in 1873, with an initial interest solely in confronting the problem of alcoholism. In the beginning, the WCTU stressed temperance alone as a solution to alcoholism, but eventually the concern was on how social conditions were responsible for alcohol's affliction upon women, society, and the family institution. The focus

of the WCTU gradually expanded, and the organization offered major political challenges as reform proposals included "prison reform, child-labor
laws, working women's protective legislation, women's suffrage, and the establishment of kindergartens."[10]

At the turn of the century, women continued to help other women
through the settlement house movement. Middle-class women established
neighborhood centers in order to communicate American culture, practical
and vocational skills, and the then-emerging "ideology of educated motherhood" to poor newcomers, many of whom were living as marginal people
in the New World.[11] Historian Allen David, in evaluating the settlement
house movement, claims that women were transformed by the involvement
itself: they evolved from being parochial volunteers to so-called
"spearheads of reform," thus changing their mode of voluntary participation
as they linked the trauma of personal transition with political shortcom-
ings.[12] One such reformer was Florence Kelley of Hull House who investigated child labor laws. Her efforts eventually led to the establishment of the
Children's Bureau in 1912.[13] Often women associated with settlement houses
initiated surveys of housing conditions and organized city planning confer-
ences. Their efforts led to the professionalization of urban concerns and the
growth of civic expertise, mainly a male field. Other women at this time entered ward politics, challenging elected officials to act as intermediary
agents on their behalf. The settlement house movement was also affiliated
closely with labor unions in the major American cities. In this period, the
famous Women's Trade Union League (WTUL) was organized by Mary
McDowell of the University of Chicago Settlement. The activities of the
WTUL included lobbying, support to striking women workers, campaigns
for protective legislation, and leadership training for women.[14] At a time
when a women's "proper place" was in the home, many women's groups
justified their reform activities by "the traditional 'woman's sphere' argument—that the moral superiority of women could be put to social use, and
that women would constitute a purifying and stabilizing influence in urban
life."[15] The "women's sphere" argument both motivated women to collective
involvement and also paved social acceptance for their public roles. Many
women, in fact, perceived their social causes as a natural extension of their
domestic and familial responsibilities. Because the maintenance of home
life was contingent on acceptable community conditions, volunteer work
translated into "municipal housecleaning."[16] Frances Willard, head of the
WCTU, wrote to woman suffragist Susan B. Anthony that "men have made a
dead failure of municipal government, just as they would have of housekeeping; and government is only housekeeping on the broadest scale."[17]
Leaders of the settlement house movement proclaimed that "running New
York is just a big housekeeping job, just like your own home, only on a larger
scale. Therefore you should be interested in city wide affairs."[18]

During the New Deal women increased their activism from the previous Progressive Era, most notably their political party involvement. The Democratic party established a Reporter Plan that sent women party workers door to door informing the masses about New Deal legislation.[19] There were about 15,000 unknown women reporters and another 60,000 nameless women precinct workers who voluntarily contributed their time, energy, and competencies to the rank and file of Roosevelt's 1936 campaign.[20] During the Roosevelt administration, numerous women were appointed to policymaking posts "partly due to the influence of Eleanor Roosevelt, who was also instrumental in convincing many women social workers to involve themselves in politics and government."[21]

Several insights can be gained from the Progressive Era and the New Deal period about the political inclinations of women. The early decades show, as Gittell and Shtob point out, that political participation was the "normal" behavior of women.[22] This contradicts the stereotypes of women as passive, apathetic, or helpless citizens. In fact, the historical record reveals the political involvement of women and their ability to influence decisions. In the early years of this nation, the political interests of its female citizens extended to urban affairs, citizen rights, and institutional maintenance. To this day, political scientists comment on the "sympathetic" or empathetic position women take on political issues.[23] Political surveys find that women are more favorably disposed than men to the achievement of racial equality and the passage of social welfare programs.[24]

Housewifery, Suburbanism, and the Role of the Citizen

In the post World War II period, women retreated to the housewife role in response to the social circumstances which patterned their lives. The history of this time records the flight of families to developing suburbs in the context of a prosperous economy along with a nationwide decline in political activism. Segregated sex roles became the norm in the family unit where the majority of women assumed the expressive, nurturant homemaker role and their husbands shouldered economic responsibility in the instrumental, breadwinning role.[25] This sexual division of labor replicated itself throughout society. Government continued to be male-dominated while women, the seemingly absent half, voted but primarily concentrated their efforts within the home.[26] Many, including political scientists, having forgotten the past, took for granted that this obscure political participation was "typical" to women as they lived out the "feminine mystique" of purpose, happiness, and success defined by husband and children.[27] However, in the 1950s, as in the Progressive Era, the women who did the volunteering were middle class while working-class women were categorized as "nonjoiners."[28] White middle-class women were the usual volunteers in civic associations, local branches of the Democratic and Republican parties, church groups, the League of Women Voters, charitable organizations, and the PTA, overall participating in a service capacity rather than politically.[29]

Service volunteering refers to the kind of charitable activities which assist the maintenance and delivery of public services. Political volunteering is directed at the changing and planning of social institutions, and requires entry into the power structure. Some argue that the service-oriented version of volunteerism was merely a convenient way of occupying time and relieving the boredom experienced by isolated, unemployed suburban women. Although the localized and noncontroversial volunteerism of women in the 1950s was subdued and did not draw national headlines, it was fundamental to the proper upkeep of residential municipalities and the working of local politics. The actions of female volunteers substantively aided the molding of the suburban dream because the value of community was reinforced thereby. Although the husbands of these suburban women belonged to a host of "community-minded" organizations, their membership was frequently motivated by career mobility.[30] The husbands were phantom citizens commuting to their jobs in the city. Community maintenance was designated as wives' work.[31]

Many women, then and now, limit their involvement to local affairs and in the eyes of society are "just volunteers." For others, however, volunteer work at the local level develops into a political career. Jeane J. Kirkpatrick, in her book *Political Woman,* discusses the career stages of forty-six women who have been elected state legislators[32] and accurately states that "where power is greater, the number of women sharply declines."[33] Women who are state legislators are among those who have gained entry into the "political class."[34] The "pathways to state power" for these women politicians were identified by Kirkpatrick.[35] The women who won public support to be lawmakers were characteristically housewives by occupation.[36] According to Kirkpatrick, "This is an unusual, unfamiliar, sex-specific pathway to political office, one virtually unexplored by political scientists."[37] Male legislators, on the other hand, typically hold careers in real estate, farming, journalism, and insurance, and more often than not are lawyers.[38]

Housewifery in and of itself, of course, did not launch these women to public office. Homemaking in combination with community involvement established a political orientation for these women. What Kirkpatrick terms "the volunteer route" or "the party worker route" was the usual avenue to the state house.[39] "Volunteer community service and volunteer political work alike provide women without special professional or educational training for a legislative career an opportunity to acquire experience, skills, and reputations that qualify them for public office."[40] Furthermore, "this aspect of volunteer work is frequently overlooked and underemphasized."[41]

Kirkpatrick's interviews with these female legislators indicate that "involvement stimulates involvement" to the point where elected public office is an expansion of the citizen role.[42] Kirkpatrick also found that the "problem-solving orientation" peculiar to local politics had been learned by these women and was appropriately transferred to state levels.[43] These legislators are examples of women who started their careers as anonymous civic and/or political party workers. Upward mobility in the political system entailed a gradual process of effort, involvement, and recognition that finally earned each woman her public name.

At the local level, women also are elected to public offices via the housewife/volunteer gender model of recruitment specified by Kirkpatrick.[44] Women who are elected or appointed to serve as judges, city council members, public commissioners, community board members, and the like more than likely rose to these recognized echelons of community decisionmaking after years of hard work in an array of area organizations.[45]

The political careers of many white, middle-class, suburban women continue to develop through volunteer work in respectable community associations. Another cohort of community-minded women, however, exists side by side and is found among lower-income women who reside in inner cities and working-class neighborhoods. This strata of women pursue an activist style of volunteering that surfaced in the radical politics of the 1960s.

Grass-Roots Politics

The politically tumultuous 1960s challenged established policies and even the very organization of government. It was a time of paramount public participation. Politics became citizen initiated and localized; advocacy groups served as important vehicles to assert issues in the civil rights movement, the women's movement, and antiwar campaigns. President Johnson's War on Poverty was influential in politicizing the city by encouraging the "maximum feasible participation" of minorities through the appropriation of community action programs. Volunteerism was transformed into a grass-roots endeavor responsive to the neighborhood emphasis in urban policy. Women were at the forefront of the poor who mobilized for the maintenance of their communities.[46]

Lower-income women assumed a community role for themselves that entailed a direct, creative participation in the policymaking process. Their legitimacy in the political system, however, was not immediate but incrementally earned, at times through confrontation politics modeled on the tactics utilized by other social movements. Women entered a dynamic interaction with officials that included bargaining, pressuring, challenging, and demonstrating in order to procure needed services, programs, and policies for their communities.[47]

This activism gave rise to a fairer distribution and adequate delivery of urban services. Political scientists Gelb and Gittell conclude that "in the 1960s, health care clinics, day care centers, after-school programs, multipurpose centers, and senior citizen programs—all based in the neighborhood and controlled by client-participants—became the new mode of urban service."[48] Furthermore, "once again, women used community organizations to press for public policies to meet the special needs of women and their families."[49] Black women at the poverty level, especially, made substantial gains in the welfare system through their involvement with the National Welfare Rights Movement (NWRM). AFDC mothers, who had organized locally (on the basis of their AFDC status) in cities throughout the United States and had developed a reputation for militancy, were ultimately influential in reforming the welfare system and securing their rights and respect as recipients.[50] Feminist goals also were realized as women set up alternative communal services designed specifically for the needs of women, such as rape crisis centers, counseling and hot line services, women's shelters for victims of violence, and community-sponsored educational programs.[51]

By the 1970s community concerns escalated into white, ethnic working-class neighborhoods—the Little Italys, the Polish Towns, and the South Sides of major U.S. cities.[52] In these urban areas resided the so-called "silent majority" who traditionally voted Democratic, paid their taxes, and took pride in their self-sufficiency as Middle Americans.[53] Women in this strata—that is, the wives of blue-collar workers—were typically homebound with a tendency to be exclusively family-centered.[54] Public references to working-class women, sometimes exaggerated in stereotypes, depicted a "personal passivity" and "worldly ineptitude" that communicated their real lack of political presence.[55]

As the crises of city living imposed upon the transitional neighborhoods of the working class, women emerged from their domesticity in defense of their ethnic enclaves. Solid working-class areas were facing a downward transformation. "An array of social and environmental issues such as housing, crime, and pollution"[56] as well as the new urban economics of gentrification, blockbusting, and redlining necessitated solutions through a system of community supports.[57] Furthermore, the lives of working-class women were being swept into the contemporary wave of change in sex roles and family form. Women's issues became personalized, and they, too, needed locally based day care centers, senior citizen centers, health clinics, counseling services, and the like.[58]

To achieve these goals, working-class women continued to enter urban politics via a community role that entails the use of assertive participatory tactics such as "lobbying, sitting on citizen committees, demonstrating, writing grants, assisting in service-oriented groups, and occasionally appearing on the evening news."[59] This grass-roots involvement of white ethnic women is widespread as evidenced by their umbrella organization, the National Congress of Neighborhood Women (NCNW), headquartered in Brooklyn with affiliates in thirty other U.S. cities.[60] Women in the NCNW form political networks both locally and nationally to maintain citizen rights, protect the environment, and assure adequate human and city service delivery from neighborhood to neighborhood in cities across the country. The NCNW evaluates the overall community effort of its membership, that is, "the wives of truck drivers, maintenance workers, policemen, and carpenters (who may themselves be clerical, service, blue-collar workers or housewives)"[61] and concludes that these women are "the unrecognized leaders in our communities."[62]

The political linkage between indigenously sponsored community groups and city hall is now the norm in urban governance. This is largely the result of the understated political efficacy demonstrated by working-class and lower-income women who can be described as "run of the mill Americans."[63] They belong to a strata in society who are "nobody special" in the power system.[64] Their political involvement has not usually transformed them into political personalities. The testimony to their politics is community betterment.

Across the country, especially in the older, industrial cities of the northeast and midwest, such as Boston, Philadelphia, Baltimore, Rochester, Chicago, Cleveland, Milwaukee, Detroit, and Cincinnati white, working-class women are constructively responding to the physical and social problems plaguing their neighborhoods. One case study of white, ethnic, working-class women and civic activism was conducted in the South St. Louis neighborhood of Carondelet.[65] Carondelet is representative of trends in the nation among neighborhoods of this type. Like many other such neighborhoods, Carondelet is an older, blue-collar area facing physical decline that requires political representation in the competitive factions of city government, and is stifled with outmoded human services.[66] The volunteerism of Carondelet women, initiated in the 1960s by a civic-oriented church group, comprises a complexity of roles. Women who volunteer are responsible for the upkeep of core community institutions such as the schools, a neighborhood medical clinic, a government-funded social action center, and a church-initiated civic betterment association; a citizen patrol squad aids the police department.[67] The routine maintenance of the community is also the work of the volunteers. For example, volunteers supported by their respective organizations pressure the city to remove blight, to install more street signs and mailboxes, or to investigate vandalized public property.[68] Volunteers have organized a large-scale housing drive requiring each homeowner in the community to individually abide by the city housing code.[69] Volunteers also have enlisted the support and participation of area residents through town meetings, circulating petitions, and lobbying trips.[70] Crisis intervention, too, is characteristic of the volunteering role in Carondelet. Women have intervened on the controversial issue of interracial school busing by mobilizing parent groups to support a city-wide lawsuit.[71] They united in successful opposition against the city's proposed development of a $12 million industrial park that threatened to raze 200 homes.[72] Long-term planning also guides the political stance of volunteers. Present-day volunteers are shaping a community of tomorrow by adhering to a conscious strategy that supports Carondelet's current status as a total community, that is a self-contained residential area which offers residents a full range of services necessary for living and for maintaining a family. Volunteers resist "progressive" innovations which in their terms means an avoidance of highways, shopping malls, high-rise office buildings, industrial parks, and apartment complexes. These volunteers intend to prevent their characteristically ethnic neighborhood from becoming a transient city locale or a suburb.[73]

In the past the working-class women of Carondelet limited their volunteer work to churches, schools, and recreational groups.[74] Changing social conditions expanded their interests to include community survival.

> Along with "sitting on boards," "staffing day care centers," and "sealing envelopes," the history of Carondelet women's citizen participation reveals that in the past they have lobbied, gone to court to testify on social issues such as discrimination, established a Montessori school, written newspaper editorials, and attended workshops pertaining to the ERA. They have even demonstrated against the development of a low-income housing project. Perhaps, the most dramatic example is the case of local women who organized an anti-pollution campaign, touring area factories, and distributing "Worst Polluter of the Year" awards. The event received televised media coverage.[75]

In urban politics the activism of minority women and white working-class women has had important political consequences. Politicians and social scientists alike have come to view the city as a collection of neighborhoods, and "the neighborhood is thus an important tool in the search for a meaningful social order in America."[76] The activism of the past several decades has led to the realization that the resolution of urban dilemmas and the quest for appropriate urban services and amenities are dependent upon a mutual exchange between residents and elected officials.[77] The massive citizen participation on the part of women, furthermore, has broken down traditional divisions in political behavior because urban politics, at least, is no longer dominated by men or the advantaged social classes.

Conclusion

The voluntary political involvement of unnamed women throughout U.S. history has helped humanize the city, and in the process has enhanced democratic channels within urban politics. Women have proven themselves to be as capable as men in taking a stand, initiating action, and successfully achieving goals related to public issues. There is, however, a unique dimension to the female experience and perspective of politics. One fact is that women's issues, issues that are usually ignored by male politicians and stand as a separate category of underrated social concerns, are given serious attention and even priority by politically involved women. Geraldine Ferraro, the Democratic party vice presidential candidate in 1984, is "terribly frustrated by what seemed to be the male indifference to women's issues."[78] Congressional policies and budget allotments, she argues, ultimately filter down to everyday realities and instigate community response.[79] Ferraro, furthermore, sees basic variation in the political psychology of the sexes. "Instead of engaging in confrontation, women were more apt to negotiate, I learned from reading Carol Gilligan's book, *In a Different Voice.* Instead of looking at short-term solutions to problems, women were more apt to think in terms of generations to come. Instead of thinking in win-lose terms, women were more apt to consider the gray areas in between."[80]

Women who volunteer generally conform to these patterns. Certainly, women can be confrontational, but their capacity for cooperative political bargaining is largely responsible for their many successful projects in community problemsolving. The political sense of women volunteers indicates their sensitivity as well to the long-term consequences of present decisions. This is made evident by the working-class women of Carondelet—they do not subscribe to random or piecemeal strategies. Instead, their volunteerism is guided by well-articulated choices in order to ensure continuity in neighborhood betterment. Volunteers in any community find politics more often than not to be an exercise in relativity rather than a discernible game of wins and losses. Those who volunteer experience their plight as one in a plurality of competing groups. Their political victories usually mean a small "piece of the pie" for their community.

Volunteerism remains important to the welfare and governance of the places in which citizens live—inner city ghettos, blue-collar communities, ethnic enclaves, the suburbs, small towns, counties, and many other kinds of localities. Volunteers address the often-forgotten needs of numerous groups, for example, women, children, the elderly, the sick, the abused, the poor. A new challenge that awaits both women and men in the "human politics" of volunteerism is the development of a nonsexist city[81]—that is, an urban area with facilities and services realistically accommodating the multiple roles played by contemporary women. There is a need for volunteers to both encourage and participate in a redesign of urban space "so it better reflects the needs of working women for more efficient transportation networks, child care, and home care services."[82]

In conclusion, volunteerism, which is integral to the governing system, and is important to the shaping of egalitarian laws and policies, also has curious implications for women's political destiny. Several women discussed in this volume who have attained national political prominence—Geraldine Ferraro, Barbara Mikulski, Margaret Heckler, and Shirley Chisholm—initiated their political careers in the volunteer sector.

Notes

1. Sandra Baxter and Marjorie Lansing, *Women and Politics: The Invisible Majority* (Ann Arbor: University of Michigan Press, 1980), 116.

2. See Bernice Cummings and Victoria Schuck, eds., *Women Organizing: An Anthology* (Metuchen, N.J.: Scarecrow Press, 1979).

3. The National Organization for Women's official statement on volunteerism is found in a booklet entitled *Volunteerism: What It's All About* (Chicago: NOW, 1971).

4. Betty Friedan, *The Second Stage* (New York: Summit Books, 1981), 323–340.

5. Innovative concepts for the organization of a democratic government are discussed by Alvin Toffler, *The Third Wave* (New York: Bantam Books, 1980), 416–443; also see Mark Satin, "Do-It Yourself Government," *Esquire* (April 1983):126–128.

6. Linda Christiansen-Ruffman, "Participation Theory and the Methodological Construction of Invisible Women: Feminism's Call for Appropriate Methodology," *Journal of Voluntary Action Research* 14 (April-September 1985):102.

7. Marilyn Gittell and Teresa Shtob, "Changing Women's Roles in Political Volunteerism and Reform of the City," *Signs* 5 (Spring 1980):S67–S78.

8. Ibid., S67.

9. Ibid., S67–S68.

10. Ibid., S69.

11. Ibid., S69–S70.

12. Allen David's thesis is discussed in ibid., S70.

13. Ibid.

14. Ibid., S70–S72.

15. Ibid., S69.

16. Friedan, *The Second Stage,* 334.

17. Gittell, "Changing Women's Roles," S69.

18. Ibid., S71.

19. Ibid., S72.

20. Ibid.

21. Ibid.

22. Ibid., S73.

23. Baxter, *Women and Politics,* 56–59.

24. Ibid., 59–60.

25. The sociological theory of traditional sex role behavior is explained by Talcott Parsons and Robert F. Bales, *Family, Socialization and Interaction Process* (New York: Free Press, 1955).

26. Gittell, "Changing Women's Roles," S72.

27. For a thorough description of the lives of women in the 1950s and the rise of feminist consciousness, see Betty Friedan, *The Feminine Mystique* (New York: Norton, 1963).

28. Gittell, "Changing Women's Roles," S73.

29. *Americans Volunteer* (Washington: Manpower Department of the U.S. Department of Labor, monograph no. 10 April 1969), 3.

30. Herbert J. Gans, The *Levittowners: Ways of Life and Politics in a New Suburban Community* (New York: Pantheon, 1967), 61.

31. Ibid., 61.

32. Jeane J. Kirkpatrick, *Political Woman* (New York: Basic Books, 1974).

33. Ibid., 21.

34. Ibid.

35. Ibid., 59.

36. Ibid., 61.

37. Ibid.

38. Ibid.

39. Ibid., 61–69.

40. Ibid., 69.

41. Ibid.

42. Ibid., 67.

43. Ibid., 65.

44. Kirkpatrick is cited in Susan Gluck Mezey, "The Effects of Sex on Recruitment: Connecticut Local Offices" in Debra W. Stewart, ed., *Women in Local Politics* (Metuchen, N.J.: Scarecrow Press, 1980), 71–72.

45. Ibid.

46. Gittell, "Changing Women's Roles," S73–S74.

47. Ibid., S74.

48. Joyce Gelb and Marilyn Gittell, "Seeking Equality: The Role of Activist Women in Cities" in Janet K. Boles, ed., *The Egalitarian City: Issues of Rights, Distribution, Access, and Power* (New York: Praeger, 1986), 97.

49. Ibid., 96.

50. Ibid., 96; Gittell, "Changing Women's Roles," 99–103.

51. Gelb, "Seeking Equality," 99–103.

52. Irene Dabrowski, "Working-Class Women in the Public Realm: Volunteerism in a St. Louis Neighborhood" in Dennis L. Thompson, ed., *The Private Exercise of Public Functions* (Port Washington, N.Y.: Associated Faculty Press, 1985), 56.

53. Ibid.

54. Ibid.

55. Ibid., 69.

56. Ibid., 57.

57. Ibid., 56.

58. Ibid., 57.

59. Ibid.

60. Ibid., 58.

61. Ibid.

62. Cited in ibid., 58; see Susan Malone and Pat Ciccone, *National Congress of Neighborhood Women Information Brochure* (Brooklyn, N.Y.: National Congress of Neighborhood Women, 1979), 1.

63. Richard Sennett and Jonathan Cobb, *The Hidden Injuries of Class* (New York: Alfred A. Knopf, 1972), 213.

64. Ibid.

65. Dabrowski, "Working-Class Women," 56–71.

66. Ibid., 60–61.

67. Ibid., 64–65.

68. Ibid., 65.

69. Ibid., 62.

70. Ibid., 62.

71. Ibid., 61.

72. Ibid.

73. Ibid., 68.

74. Ibid., 64.

75. Ibid., 63.

76. Sandra Perlman Schoenberg and Patricia L. Rosenbaum, *Neighborhoods That Work: Sources for Viability in the Inner City* (New Brunswick, N.J.: Rutgers University Press, 1980), 146.

77. See Irene J. Dabrowski, Anthony L. Haynor, and Robert F. Cuervo, "An Exchange Approach to Community Politics: A Case Study of White Ethnic Activism in Staten Island, New York" in Boles, *The Egalitarian City,* 110–128.

78. Geraldine A. Ferraro with Linda Bird Francke, *Ferraro: My Story* (New York: Bantam Books, 1985), 43.

79. Ibid., 132–137.

80. Ibid., 57; also see Carol Gilligan, *In A Different Voice: Psychological Theory and Women's Development* (Cambridge, Mass.: Harvard University Press, 1982).

81. Gelb, "Seeking Equality," 107.

82. Ibid., 106.

Selected Bibliography

FRANK P. Le VENESS

The following bibliography contains representative entries of books and articles concerning American women in politics which were published during the 1970s and 1980s. Readers are reminded that further bibliographical materials may be found in a number of the books listed below, including listings of works published during earlier periods.

Books

The books listed below contain information concerning a wide range of matters of political interest and concern to American women. Many also discuss in depth economic and social issues, which in turn often have political ramifications. The listing is intended to offer readers a wide sampling of viewpoints and research endeavors.

Attention should be drawn to three bibliographic items of particular note for readers:

Morris Levitt. *Dissertations in Political Science on Women*. Monticello, Illinois: Vance Bibliographies, 1982.
Kathy Stanwick and Christine Li. *The Political Participation of Women in the United States: A Selected Bibliography, 1950–1976*. Metuchen, New Jersey: Scarecrow Press, 1977.
Ina J. Weis. *Women in Politics*. Monticello: Vance Bibliographies, 1979.

General Books

Abbott, Delila M. *Women Legislators of Utah, 1896–1976*. Salt Lake City: Utah Chapter, Order of Women Legislators, 1976.
Amundsen, Kirsten. *The Silenced Majority: Women and American Democracy*. Englewood Cliffs, New Jersey: Prentice-Hall, 1971.
———. *A New Look at the Silenced Majority: Women and American Democracy*. Englewood Cliffs: Prentice-Hall, 1977.
Andreas, Carol. *Sex and Caste in America*. Englewood-Cliffs: Prentice-Hall, 1971.
Anticaglia, Elizabeth. *A Housewife's Guide to Women's Liberation*. Chicago: Nelson-

Hall, 1972.

Barber, James David, and Barbara Kellerman, eds. *Women Leaders in American Politics.* Englewood Cliffs: Prentice-Hall, 1986.

Baxter, Sandra, and Marjorie Lansing. *Women and Politics: The Invisible Majority.* Ann Arbor: University of Michigan Press, 1980.

Bernard, Jessie Shirley. *Women and the Public Interest: An Essay on Policy and Protest.* Chicago: Aldine, Atherton, 1971.

Blair, Karen J. *The Clubwoman as Feminist.* New York: Holmes and Meier, 1980.

Boles, Janet K., ed. *The Egalitarian City: Issues of Rights, Distribution, Access, and Power.* New York: Praeger, 1986. (Note chapter: Irene Dabrowski, Anthony L. Haynor, and Robert F. Cuervo. "An Exchange Approach to Community Policies: A Case Study of White Ethnic Activism in Staten Island, New York.")

Butler, Phyllis, and Dorothy Gray. *Everywoman's Guide to Political Awareness.* Millbrae, California: Les Femmes, 1976.

Carroll, Susan J. *Women as Candidates in American Politics.* Bloomington: Indiana University Press, 1985.

Center for American Women and Politics, Rutgers University. *Women in Public Office: A Biographical Directory and Statistical Analysis.* New York: R. R. Bowker, 1976 and Metuchen: Scarecrow Press, 1978.

Chamberlain, Hope. *A Minority of Members: Women in the U.S. Congress.* New York: Praeger, 1973.

Davison, Jaquie. *I Am a Housewife!* New York: Guild Books, 1972.

Decter, Midge. *The Liberated Woman and Other Americans.* New York: Coward, McCann, and Geoghegan, 1971.

———. *The New Chastity and Other Arguments against Women's Liberation.* New York: Coward, McCann, and Geoghegan, 1972.

Doyle, Nancy. *Woman's Changing Place: A Look at Sexism.* New York: Public Affairs Committee, 1974.

Editorial Research Reports on the Women's Movement. Washington, D.C.: *Congressional Quarterly,* 1973.

Englebarts, Rudolf. *Women in the United States Congress, 1917–1972: Their Accomplishments with Bibliographies.* Littleton, Colorado: Libraries Unlimited, 1974.

Federation of Organizations for Professional Women. *Washington Women.* Washington, D.C.: 1978.

Feldman, Sylvia D. *The Rights of Women.* Rochelle Park, New Jersey: Hayden Books, 1974.

Ferriss, Abbott L. *Indicators of Trends in the Status of American Women.* New York: Russell Sage Foundation, 1974.

Flammang, Janet A., ed. *Political Women: Current Roles in State and Local Government.* Beverly Hills, California: Sage Publications, 1984. (*Sage Yearbooks in Women's Policy Studies,* Vol. 8.)

Flexner, Eleanor. *Century of Struggle: The Woman's Rights Movement in the United States.* rev. ed. Cambridge: Belknap Press of Harvard University Press, 1975.

———. *Women's Rights—An Unfinished Business.* New York: Public Affairs Committee, 1971.

Freeman, Jo, ed. *Women: A Feminist Perspective.* 3d ed. Palo Alto, California: Mayfield, 1984. (Note: Naomi B. Lynn has written an article for each edition: first, "Women and Politics: An Overview" [1972]; second, "American Women and the Political Process" [1975]; and third, "Women and Politics: The Real Majority.")

Friedan, Betty. *The Second Stage.* New York: Summit Books, 1981.

Gelb, Joyce, and Marian Lief Palley. *Women and Public Policies.* Princeton, New Jersey: Princeton University Press, 1982.

Gertzog, Irwin N. *Congressional Women.* New York: Praeger, 1984.

Githens, Marianne, and Jewel L. Prestage, eds. *A Portrait of Marginality: The Political Behavior of American Women.* New York: D. McKay, 1977. (Note: Naomi B. Lynn and Cornelia Flora wrote a chapter, "Societal Punishment and Aspects of Female Political Participation.")

Gould, Elsie M., comp. *American Woman Today: Free or Frustrated?* Englewood Cliffs: Prentice-Hall, 1972.

Graebner, Allan. *After Eve: The New Feminism.* Minneapolis: Augsburg Publishing House, 1972.

Gruborg, Martin. *Women in American Politics: An Assessment and Sourcebook.* Oshkosh, Wisconsin: Academia Press, 1968.

Hawks, Joanne V., and Shiela L. Skemp, eds. *Sex, Race and the Role of Women in the South.* Jackson: University Press of Mississippi, 1983.

Hecht, Marie B., *et al. The Women Yes!* New York: Holt, Rinehart and Winston, 1973. Reprinted by R. E. Krieger, 1979.

Hewlett, Sylvia Ann. *A Lesser Life: The Myth of Women's Liberation in America.* New York: William Morrow, 1986.

Hole, Judith, and Ellen Levine. *The Rebirth of Feminism.* New York: Quadrangle Books, 1971.

Howard, Jane. *A Different Woman.* New York: Dutton, 1973.

Jaquette, Jane S., ed. *Women in Politics.* New York: John Wiley and Sons, 1974. (Naomi Lynn and Cornelia Flora wrote the chapter "Women and Political Socialization: Consideration on the Impact of Motherhood.")

Jensen, Joan M. *Loosening the Bonds.* New Haven, Connecticut: Yale University Press, 1986.

Kelly, Rita Mae, and Mary Boutillier. *The Making of Political Women: A Study of Socialization and Role Conflict.* Chicago: Nelson-Hall, 1978.

Kendrigan, Mary-Lou. *Political Equality in a Democracy Society: Women in the United States.* Contribution in Women's Studies. No. 45. Westport, Connecticut: Greenwood Press, 1984.

Klein, Ethel. *Gender Politics: From Consciousness to Mass Politics.* Cambridge: Harvard University Press, 1984.

Kohn, Walter. *Women in National Legislatures.* New York: Praeger, 1980.

Lamson, Peggy. *Few Are Chosen: American Women in Political Life Today.* Boston: Houghton-Mifflin, 1970.

————. *In the Vanguard: Six American Women in Public Life.* Boston: Houghton-Mifflin, 1979. (Note chapter on the then Congresswoman Elizabeth Holtzman.)

Leahy, Margaret. *Development Strategies and the Status of Women: A Comparative Study of the United States, Mexico, the Soviet Union, and Cuba.* Boulder, Colorado: Lynne Rienner, 1986.

Lee, Essie E. *Women in Congress.* New York: Julian Messner, 1979.

Lynn, Naomi B., and Rita Mae Kelly, eds. *United Nations Decade for Women World Conference.* New York: The Haworth Press, 1984. (Note Naomi B. Lynn article "The National Women's Decade: Equality, Women and Peace.")

Marine, Gene. *A Male Guide to Women's Liberation.* New York: Holt, Rinehart and Winston, 1972.

Marlow, H. Carleton, and Harrison M. Davis. *The American Search for Woman.* Santa Barbara, California: CLIO Books, 1976.

Millett, Kate. *Sexual Politics.* Garden City, New York: Doubleday, 1970.

Morgan, David. *Suffragists and Democrats: The Politics of Woman Suffrage in America.* East Lansing: Michigan State University Press, 1971.

Okin, Susan Moller. *Women in Political Thought.* Princeton: Princeton University Press, 1979.

Randall, Vicky. *Women and Politics.* London: Mackays of Chatham, Macmillan Press, 1982.

Rendel, Margherita, and Georgina Ashworth, eds. *Women, Power and Political Systems.* New York: St. Martin's Press, 1981.

Republican Party, National Committee, 1968–1972, Women's Division. *Women in Public Service.* Washington, D.C.: 1971.

Robbins, Joan. In *Handbook of Women's Liberation.* Roger Lovin, ed. North Hollywood, California: Now Library Press, 1970.

Rossi, Alice S. *Feminists in Politics: A Panel Analysis of the First National Women's Conference.* New York: Academic Press, 1982. (Note: Conference held in Houston, Texas, June, 1977.)

Safilios-Rothschild, Constantina. *Women and Social Policy.* Englewood Cliffs: Prentice-Hall, 1974.

Sapiro, Virginia. *The Political Integration of Women: Roles, Socialization, and Politics.* Champaign: University of Illinois Press, 1983.

Sawer, Marian. *A Woman's Place.* Boston: Allen and Unwin, 1984.

Schlafly, Phyllis. *The Power of the Positive Woman.* New Rochelle, New York: Arlington House, 1977.

Sheldon, Suzanne Eaton. *Women in Government.* Lincolnwood, Illinois: VGM Career Horizons, 1983.

Siddon, Sally Goodyear. *Consider Yourself for Public Office.* Washington, D.C.: National Federation of Republican Women, 1976.

Siltanen, Janet, and Michelle Stanworth. *Women and the Public Sphere: A Critique of Sociology and Politics.* New York: St. Martin's Press, 1984.

Smeal, Eleanor. *Why and How Women Will Elect the Next President.* New York: Harper and Row, 1984.

Sochen, June. *Movers and Shakers: American Women Thinkers and Activists, 1900–1970.* New York: Quadrangle Books, 1973.

Stacey, Margaret. *Women, Power, and Politics.* New York: Tavistock, 1981.

Stewart, Debra. *Women in Local Politics.* Metuchen: Scarecrow Press, 1980.

Stineman, Esther. *American Political Women: Contemporary and Historical Profiles.* Littleton, Colorado: Libraries Unlimited, 1980.

Tinker, Irene. *Women in Washington: Advocates for Public Policy.* Beverly Hills:

Sage Publications, 1983.

Tolchin, Susan, and Martin Tolchin. *Clout: Womanpower and Politics.* New York: Coward, McCann and Geoghegan, 1973.

Trafton, Barbara M. *Women Winning: How to Run for Political Office.* Boston: Harvard Common Press, 1984.

Tuchman, Gaye, Arlene Kaplan Daniels, and James Benet. *Hearth and Home: Images of Women in the Mass Media.* New York: Oxford University Press, 1978.

United States, Executive Office of the President. *Women: A Documentary of Progress During the Administration of Jimmy Carter, 1977 to 1981.* Washington, D.C.: 1981.

United States National Commission for UNESCO. *Report on Women in America.* Washington, D.C.: 1977.

Ware, Celestine. *Women Power: The Movement for Women's Liberation.* New York: Tower, 1970.

Williams, Barbara. *Breakthrough: Women in Politics.* New York: Walker, 1979.

Women in Congress, 1917–1976. Washington, D.C.: U.S. Government Printing Office, 1976.

Biographies, Autobiographies, and Books Written by U.S. Women in Politics

Abzug, Bella. *Gender Gap: Bella Abzug's Guide to Political Power for American Women.* Boston: Houghton-Mifflin, 1984.

———. *Ms. Abzug Goes to Washington.* New York: Saturday Review Press, 1972.

Breslin, Rosemary, and Joshua Hammer. *Gerry!: A Woman Making History.* New York: Pinnacle Books, 1984.

Chisholm, Shirley. *The Good Fight.* New York: Harper and Row, 1973.

———. *Unbought and Unbossed.* Boston: Houghton-Mifflin, 1970.

Ferraro, Geraldine, with Linda Bird Francke. *Ferraro, My Story.* New York: Bantam Books, 1985.

Haskins, James. *Barbara Jordan.* New York: Dial Press, 1977.

———. *Fighting Shirley Chisholm.* New York: Dial Press, 1975.

Kirkpatrick, Jeane J., *Dictatorships and Double Standards: Rationalism and Reason in Politics.* New York: The American Enterprise Institute and Simon and Schuster, 1982.

———. *The New Presidential Elite: Men and Women in National Politics.* New York: Twentieth Century Fund and Russell Sage Foundation, 1976.

———. *Political Woman.* New York: Basic Books, 1974.

———. *The Reagan Phenomenon: And Other Speeches on Foreign Policy.* Washington, D.C.: The American Institute for Public Policy Research, 1983.

Katz, Lee Michael. *My Name is Geraldine Ferraro: An Unauthorized Biography.* New York: New American Library, 1984.

Lyness, Jack. "Margaret M. Heckler, Republican Representative from Massachusetts." In Ralph Nader, *Citizens Look at Congress.* Washington, D.C.: Grossman, 1972.

Mohr, Lillian Holmen. *Frances Perkins: That Woman in FDR's Cabinet!* Croton-on-Hudson, New York: North River Press, 1979.

Articles

The articles listed below, also from the period since 1970, are generally restricted to those pertaining directly to the candidacy and election of women in American politics. However, they also include some articles written by authors of this book which concern other aspects of women and politics.

Readers' attention is drawn to two special issues of journals which were devoted exclusively to women's issues:

Boneparth, Ellen, ed. "Special Issue on Women and Politics." *The Western Political Quarterly.* Vol. 34, No. 1 (March 1981).

Clark, Janet M., ed. "Women in State and Local Politics." *The Social Science Journal.* Vol. 21, No. 1 (January 1984).

Ambrosius, Margery M., and Susan Welch. "Women and Politics at the Grassroots: Women Candidates for State Office in Three States, 1950–1978." *The Social Science Journal* Vol. 21, No. 1 (January 1984): 29–40.

Anderson, Kristi, and Stuart Thorson. "Congressional Turnover and the Election of Women." *The Western Political Quarterly* Vol. 37, No. 1 (March 1984): 143–56.

Baer, Denise L., and John S. Jackson. "Are Women Really More 'Amateur' in Politics than Men?" *Women and Politics* Vol. 5 (Summer-Fall 1985): 79–92.

Benze, James G., Jr., and Eugene R. Declercq. "Content of Television Political Spot Ads for Female Candidates." *Journalism Quarterly* Vol. 62 (Summer 1985): 278–83 + .

———. "The Importance of Gender in Congressional and Statewide Elections." *The Social Science Quarterly* Vol. 66, No. 4 (December 1985): 954–63.

Bernstein, Robert A. "Why are There so Few Women in the House?" *The Western Political Quarterly* Vol. 39, No. 1 (March 1986): 155–64.

Bernstein, Robert A., and Jayne D. Polly. "Race, Class and Support for Female Candidates." *The Western Political Quarterly* Vol. 28, No. 4 (December 1975): 733–36.

Bers, Trudy Haffron. "Local Political Elites: Men and Women on Boards of Education." *The Western Political Quarterly* Vol. 31, No. 3 (September 1978): 381–91.

"Black Women and Social Change." Seminar proceedings, in *TransAfrica Forum* Vol. 2 (Summer 1983): 34–62.

Bolce, Louis. "The Role of Gender in Recent Presidential Elections: Reagan and the Reverse Gender Gap." *Presidential Studies Quarterly* Vol. 15, No. 2 (Spring 1985): 372–85.

Boles, Janet K. "The Texas Woman in Politics: Role Model or Mirage?" *The Social Science Journal* Vol. 21, No. 1 (January 1984): 79–90.

Boneparth, Ellen. "Women and Politics: Introduction." *The Western Political Quarterly* Vol. 34, No. 1 (March 1981): 3–4.

———. "Women in Campaigns: From Lickin' and Stickin' to Strategy." *American Politics Quarterly* Vol. 5, No. 3 (July 1977): 289–300.

Bourque, Susan C., and Jean Grossholtz. "Politics as an Unnatural Practice." *Politics and Society* Vol. 4, No. 2 (Winter 1974): 225–66.

Buchanan, Christopher. "Why Aren't There More Women in Congress?" *Congressional Quarterly Weekly Report* Vol. 36, No. 32 (August 12, 1978): 2108–10.

Bullock, Charles S., III, and Loch K. Johnson. "Sex and the Second Primary." *The Social Science Quarterly* Vol. 66, No. 4 (December 1985): 933–44.

Burrell, Barbara C. "Women's and Men's Campaigns for the U.S. House of Representatives, 1972–1982: A Finance Gap?" *American Politics Quarterly* Vol. 13, No. 3 (July 1985): 251–72.

Carroll, Susan J. "Political Elites and Sex Differences in Political Ambition: A Reconsideration." *The Journal of Politics* Vol. 47, No. 4 (November 1985): 1231–44.

———. "The Recruitment for Cabinet-Level Posts in State Government: A Social Control Perspective." *The Social Science Journal* Vol. 21, No. 1 (January 1984): 91–108.

———. "Women Candidates and Support for Feminist Concerns: The Closet Feminist Syndrome." *The Western Political Quarterly* Vol. 37, No. 2 (June 1984): 307–23.

Christy, Carol. A. "American and German Trends in Sex Differences in Political Participation." *Comparative Political Studies* Vol. 18, No. 1 (April 1985): 81–103.

Clark, Cal, and Janet Clark. "The Growth of Women's Candidates for Nontraditional Political Offices in New Mexico." *The Social Science Journal* Vol. 21, No. 1 (January 1984): 57–66.

Clark, Janet. "Women in State and Local Politics: Progress or Stalemate?" *The Social Science Quarterly* Vol. 21, No. 1 (January 1984): 1–4.

Clifford, Julie, and John Hanson. "Elizabeth Holtzman: New York City's First Woman District Attorney." *American Politics* (January 1984).

Costain, Anne N. "Representing Women: The Transition from Social Movement to Interest Group." *The Western Political Quarterly* Vol. 34, No. 1 (March 1981): 100–13.

Constantini, Edmond, and Kenneth H. Craik. "Women as Politicians: The Social Background, Personality, and Political Careers of Female Party Leaders." *The Journal of Social Issues* Vol. 28, No. 2 (1972): 217–36.

Dabrowski, Irene. "Working-Class Women and Civic Action: A Case Study of an Innovative Community Role." *Policy Studies Journal* Vol. 11, No. 3 (March 1983): 427–35.

———. "Working-Class Women in the Public Realm: Volunteerism in a St. Louis Neighborhood." In *The Private Exercise of Public Functions,* Dennis L. Thompson, ed. Port Washington, New York: Associated Faculty Press, 1985. 56–71.

———. "The Social Integration of Working-Class Women: A Review of Employment, Voluntary Organization, and Related Sex Role Literature." *The Social Science Journal* Vol. 21, No. 4 (October 1984): 59–73.

Darcy, Robert, Margaret Brewer, and Judy Clay. "Women in the Oklahoma Political System: State Legislative Elites." *The Social Science Journal* Vol. 21, No. 1 (January 1984): 67–78.

Darcy, R., Susan Welch, and Janet Clark. "Women Candidates in Single- and Multimember Districts: American State Legislative Races." *The Social Science Quarterly* Vol. 66, No. 4 (December 1985): 945–53.

Deber, Raisa B. "'The Fault, Dear Brutus': Women as Congressional Candidates in Pennsylvania." *The Journal of Politics* Vol. 44, No. 2 (May 1982): 463–79.

Ekstrand, Laurie F., and William A. Eckert. "The Impact of Candidate's Sex on Voter Choice." *The Western Political Quarterly* Vol. 34, No. 1 (March 1981): 78–87.

Evans, Judith. "Women in Politics: A Reappraisal." *Political Studies* Vol. 28, No. 2 (June 1980): 210–21.

Ferree, Myra Marx. "A Woman for President? Changing Responses: 1958–1972." *Public Opinion Quarterly* Vol. 38 (Fall 1974): 390–99.

Flammang, Janet A. "Female Officials in the Feminist Capital: The Case of Santa Clara County." *The Western Political Quarterly* Vol. 38, No. 1 (March 1985): 94–118.

Fowlkes, Diane L. "Women in Georgia Electoral Politics: 1970–1978." *The Social Science Journal* Vol. 21, No. 1 (January 1984): 43–56.

Fowlkes, Diane L., Jerry Perkins, and George E. Marcus. "Gender Roles and Party Roles." *The American Political Science Review* Vol. 73, No. 3 (Summer 1979): 772–80.

Frankovic, Kathleen A. "Sex and Voting in the U.S. House of Representatives, 1961–1975." *American Politics Quarterly* Vol. 5, No. 3 (July 1977): 315–30.

Fulenwider, Claire Knoche. "Feminist Ideology and the Political Attitudes and Participation of White and Minority Women." *The Western Political Quarterly* Vol. 34, No. 1 (March 1981): 17–30.

Gertzog, Irwin N. "Matrimonial Connection: The Norm of Congressmen's Widows for the House of Representatives." *The Journal of Politics* Vol. 42, No. 3 (August 1980): 820–33.

Gertzog, Irwin N., and M. Michelle Simard. "Women and 'Hopeless' Congressional Candidacies: Nomination Frequency, 1916–1978." *American Politics Quarterly* Vol. 9, No. 4 (October 1981): 449–66.

Glenney, Daryl. "Women in Politics: On the Rise." *Campaigns and Elections* Vol. 2 (Winter 1982): 18–24.

Gruberg, Martin. "From Nowhere to Where? Women in State and Local Politics." *The Social Science Journal* Vol. 21, No. 1 (January 1984): 5–12.

Hansen, Susan B., Linda M. Franz, and Margaret Netemeyer-Mays. "Women's Political Participation and Policy Preferences." *The Social Science Quarterly* Vol. 56, No. 4 (March 1976): 576–90.

Hill, David B. "Women State Legislators and Party Voting on the ERA." *The Social Science Quarterly* Vol. 64, No. 2 (June 1983): 318–26.

Holtzman, Elizabeth. "Through Their Struggle for Equality, Women Can Create a More Humanitarian Society." *Radcliffe Quarterly* (September 1983).

Jennings, M. Kent, and Barbara G. Farah. "Social Roles and Political Resources: An Over-Time Study of Men and Women in Party Elites." *American Journal of Political Science* Vol. 25, No. 3 (August 1981): 462–82.

Johannes, John R. "Women as Congressional Staffers: Does It Make a Difference?" *Women in Politics* Vol. 4 (Summer 1984): 69–81.

Kincaid, Dianna D. "Over His Dead Body: A Positive Perspective on Widows in the U.S. Congress." *The Western Political Quarterly* Vol. 31, No. 1 (March 1978): 96–104.

King, Mae C. "Oppression and Power: The Unique Status of the Black Woman in the American Political System." *The Social Science Quarterly* Vol. 56, No. 1 (June 1975): 129–42.

Knapp, Elaine B. "A Woman's Place is in the Capitol." *State Government News* Vol. 27, No. 9 (September 1984): 4–9.

Lee, Marcia Manning. "Why Few Women Hold Public Office: Democracy and Sexual Roles." *The Political Science Quarterly* Vol. 91, No. 2 (Summer 1976): 297–314.

Lynn, Naomi B. "Lost in the Management Jungle: Women and Administrative Theory." In Thomas Vocino and Richard Heimovics, editors, *Public Administration Education in Transition,* New York: Marcel Dekker, 1982. 27–35.

———. "Women, Research and Structural Realities." *Praxis* Vol. 2, No. 2 (Spring 1977).

Lynn, Naomi B., and Cornelia Flora. "Motherhood and Political Participation: The Changing Sense of Self." *Journal of Military and Political Science* (August 1973): 91–103.

Lynn, Naomi B., Allene Vaden, and Richard Vaden. "The Challenges of Men in a Woman's World." *Public Personnel Management.* Vol. 4, No. 1 (January-February 1975): 12–17.

Lynn, Naomi B., and Richard E. Vaden. "Toward A Non-Sexist Personnel Opportunity Structure: The Federal Executive Bureaucracy." *Public Personnel Management* Vol. 8, No. 4 (July-August 1979): 209–15.

Main, Eleanor C., Gerard S. Gryski, and Beth S. Shapiro. "Different Perspectives: Southern State Legislators' Attitudes about Women in Politics." *The Social Science Journal* Vol. 21, No. 1 (January 1984): 21–28.

McDonald, Jean Graves, and Vicky Howell Pierson. "Female County Party Leaders and the Perception of Discrimination: A Test of the Male Conspiracy Theory." *The Social Science Journal* Vol. 21, No. 1 (January 1984): 13–20.

McGrath, Wilma E., and John W. Soule. "Rocking the Cradle or Rocking the Boat: Women at the 1972 Democratic National Convention." *The Social Science Quarterly* Vol. 55, No. 1 (June 1974): 141–50.

McManus, Susan A. "A City's First Female Officeholder: 'Coattails' for Future Female Officeholders." *The Western Political Quarterly* Vol. 34, No. 1 (March 1981): 88–99.

Mezey, Susan Gluck. "Does Sex Make a Difference?: A Case Study of Women in Politics." *The Western Political Quarterly* Vol. 31, No. 4 (December 1978): 492–501.

Mollison, Andrew. "Widening the Gender Gap." *New Leader* Vol. 66, No. 4 (July 11–25, 1983): 3–4.

Nechemas, Carol. "Geographic Mobility: Women's Access to State Legislatures." *The Western Political Quarterly* Vol. 38, No. 1 (March 1985): 119–31.

Norris, Pippa. "The Gender Gap in Britain and America." *Parliamentary Affairs* (London) Vol. 38, No. 2 (Spring 1985): 192–201.

Perkins, Jerry, and Diane Fowlkes. "Opinion Representation Versus Social Representation: or Why Women Can't Run as Women and Win?" *The American Political Science Review* Vol. 74, No. 1 (March 1980): 92–103.

Powell, Linda Watts, Clifford W. Brown, Jr., and Roman B. Hedges. "Male and Female Differences in Elite Political Participation: An Examination of the Effects of Socio-economic and Familial Variables." *The Western Political Quarterly* Vol. 34, No. 1 (March 1981): 31–45.

Rosen, Jane. "The Kirkpatrick Factor." *The New York Times Magazine* (April 28, 1985):

48–54.

Rossi, Alice S. "Beyond the Gender Gap: Women's Bid for Political Power." *The Social Science Quarterly* Vol. 64, No. 4 (December 1983): 718–33.

Rule, Wilma. "Why Women Don't Run: The Critical Contextual Factors in Women's Legislative Recruitment." *The Western Political Quarterly* Vol. 34, No. 1 (March 1981): 60–77.

Sacket, Victoria. "Color Me Political: Changing Fashions in Women's Magazines." *Public Opinion* Vol. 7 (August-September 1984): 12–15 +.

Saltzstein, Grace Hall. "Female Mayors and Women in Municipal Jobs." *The American Journal of Political Science* Vol. 30, No. 1 (February 1986): 140–64.

Schramm, Sarah Slavin. "When Women Run Against Men." *Public Opinion Quarterly* Vol. 41, No. 1 (Spring 1977): 1–12.

———. "Women and Representation: Self-Government and Role Change." *The Western Political Quarterly* Vol. 34, No. 1 (March 1981): 46–59.

Schreiber, E. M. "Education and Change in American Opinions on a Woman for President." *Public Opinion Quarterly* Vol. 42, No. 2 (Summer 1978): 171–82.

Shapiro, Robert V. "Gender Differences in Policy Preferences: A Summary of Trends from the 1960s to the 1980s." *Public Opinion Quarterly* Vol. 50, No. 1 (Spring 1986): 42–61.

Sigelman, Carol K., Dan B. Thomas, Lee Sigelman, and Frederick D. Ribich. "Gender, Physical Attractiveness, and Electability: An Experimental Investigation of Voter Biases." *The Journal of Applied Social Psychology* Vol. 16, No. 3 (1986): 229–48.

Sigelman, Lee. "The Curious Case of Women in State and Local Government." *The Social Science Quarterly* Vol. 56, No. 4 (March 1976): 591–604.

Sigelman, Lee, and Susan Welch. "Race, Gender, and Opinion toward Black and Female Presidential Candidates." *Public Opinion Quarterly* Vol. 48, No. 2 (Summer 1984): 467–75.

Thompson, Joan Hulse. "Career Convergence: Election of Women and Men to the House of Representatives: 1916–1975." *Women and Politics* Vol. 5 (Spring 1985): 69–90.

———. "Role Perceptions of Women in the Ninety-fourth Congress, 1975–1976." *The Political Science Quarterly* Vol. 95, No. 1 (Spring 1980): 71–82.

Uhlaner, Carol Jean, and Kay Lehman Schlozman. "Candidate Gender and Congressional Campaign Receipts." *The Journal of Politics* Vol. 48, No. 1 (Fall 1986): 30–50.

Van Hightower, Nikki R. "The Recruitment of Women for Public Office." *American Politics Quarterly* Vol. 5, No. 3 (July 1977): 301–14.

Volgy, Thomas J., John E. Schwartz, and Hildy Gottleib. "Female Representation and the Quest for Resources: Feminist Activism and Electoral Success." *The Social Science Quarterly* Vol. 67, No. 1 (March 1986): 156–68.

Volgy, Thomas J., and Sandra S. Volgy. "Women and Politics: Political Correlates of Sex Role Acceptance." *The Social Science Quarterly* Vol. 55, No. 4 (March 1975): 967–74.

Welch, Susan. "Recruitment of Women to Political Office: A Discriminant Analysis." *The Western Political Quarterly* Vol. 31, No. 3 (September 1978): 372–80.

Welch, Susan, Margery M. Abrosius, Janet Clark, and Robert Darcy. "The Effect of Candidate Gender on Electoral Outcomes in State Legislative Races: A Research Note." *The Western Political Quarterly* Vol. 38, No. 3 (September 1985): 464–75.

Welch, Susan, and Philip Secret. "Sex, Race and Political Participation." *The Western Political Quarterly* Vol. 34, No. 1 (March 1981): 5–16.

Welch, Susan, and Lee Sigelman, "Changes in Public Attitudes towards Women in Politics." *The Social Science Quarterly* Vol. 63, No. 2 (June 1982): 312–22.

Whalen, James R. "Jeanne Kirkpatrick: Ideals Come First." *The Saturday Evening Post* Vol. 256, No. 9 (December 1984): 50–55.

Wickendon, Dorothy. "What Now for the Women's Movement?" *The New Republic* Vol. 194, No. 18 (May 5, 1986): 19–25.

Wilhite, Allen, and John Theilmann. "Women, Blacks, and PAC Discrimination." *The Social Science Quarterly* Vol. 67, No. 2 (June 1986): 283–98.

Zipp, John F., and Eric Pultzer. "Gender Differences in Voting for Female Candidates: Evidence from the 1982 Election." *Public Opinion Quarterly* Vol. 49, No. 2 (Summer 1985): 179–97.

Contributors

Kirsten Amundsen is the author of *The Silenced Majority: Women and American Democracy* and *A New Look at the Silenced Majority*. Recently, her research has focused on security issues; her major publication in this area is *Norway and NATO: The Forgotten Soviet Challenge*. Dr. Amundsen is a professor of government at California State University at Sacramento.

Arthur A. Belonzi is a professor of history at the Academy of Aeronautics in New York. He is author of *The Weary Watchdogs* and editor and advisor for the *American History Reader*.

Joseph C. Bertolini received his Ph.D. from New York University and is currently an adjunct assistant professor of politics at St. John's University in New York.

Reba Carruth is market research coordinator for Honeywell Europe, in Brussels. Dr. Carruth has taught at St. Cloud State University and received the 1986 International Youth and Achievement Award from the International Biographical Center in Cambridge, England.

Irene J. Dabrowski is a contributing author to *Private Exercise of Public Functions* and to *The Egalitarian City*. She is an associate professor of sociology at the Staten Island campus of St. John's University.

Arthur J. Hughes is chair of the Department of Political Science, History, and Social Studies at St. Francis College in Brooklyn, New York. Dr. Hughes is author of a biography of Richard Nixon, and a study of the American presidency. His text, *American Government,* is in its fourth edition.

Frank P. Le Veness is chair of the department of Government and Politics at St. John's University, where he has taught since 1966. Dr. Le Veness specializes in development politics and minority politics, and in Caribbean and Latin American political development. The Caribbean Studies Association presented him with its Meritorious Service Award in 1985, and St. John's

University has awarded him the Pietas Medal and the Faculty Outstanding Achievement Medal.

Orma Linford has taught at the University of Wisconsin, Beloit College, and the University of Northern Illinois, and is presently an associate professor of political science at Kansas State University. Her research has appeared in books, law reviews, and other journals.

Naomi B. Lynn has written articles and books on public administration, political science, and women and politics. She is dean of the College of Public and Urban Affairs at Georgia State University.

Vivian Jenkins Nelsen is director of administration at the Hubert H. Humphrey Institute of Public Affairs at the University of Minnesota. She is author of *Understanding Third World Women, Combatting Racism,* and *Combatting Sexism.*

Linda K. Richter is on the women's studies faculty and is associate professor of political science at Kansas State University. While a Fulbright scholar, she wrote *Land Reform and Tourism Development: Policy-Making in the Philippines* and has written numerous articles on women in developing nations, tourism politics, and Philippine politics.

Jane P. Sweeney teaches at St. John's University. She is the author of *The First European Elections: Neo-functionalism and the European Parliament.* Currently, she is a member of the editorial committee of the *Encyclopedia of the European Community* and is coediting two books: a comparative study of policies regarding terrorism and a reassessment of regional integration theory.